Number 139
Fall 2013

New Directions for Evaluation

Paul R. Brandon
Editor-in-Chief

Data Visualization, Part 1

Tarek Azzam
Stephanie Evergreen
Editors

DATA VISUALIZATION, PART 1
Tarek Azzam, Stephanie Evergreen (eds.)
New Directions for Evaluation, no. 139
Paul R. Brandon, Editor-in-Chief

Microfilm copies of issues and articles are available in 16mm and 35mm, as well as microfiche in 105mm, through University Microfilms Inc., 300 North Zeeb Road, Ann Arbor, MI 48106-1346.

New Directions for Evaluation is indexed in Education Research Complete (EBSCO Publishing), ERIC: Education Resources Information Center (CSC), Higher Education Abstracts (Claremont Graduate University), SCOPUS (Elsevier), Social Services Abstracts (ProQuest), Sociological Abstracts (ProQuest), and Worldwide Political Science Abstracts (ProQuest).

NEW DIRECTIONS FOR EVALUATION (ISSN 1097-6736, electronic ISSN 1534-875X) is part of The Jossey-Bass Education Series and is published quarterly by Wiley Subscription Services, Inc., A Wiley Company, at Jossey-Bass, One Montgomery Street, Suite 1200, San Francisco, CA 94104-4594.

SUBSCRIPTIONS for individuals cost $89 for U.S./Canada/Mexico; $113 international. For institutions, $334 U.S.; $374 Canada/Mexico; $408 international. Electronic only: $89 for individuals all regions; $334 for institutions all regions. Print and electronic: $98 for individuals in the U.S., Canada, and Mexico; $122 for individuals for the rest of the world; $387 for institutions in the U.S.; $427 for institutions in Canada and Mexico; $461 for institutions for the rest of the world.

EDITORIAL CORRESPONDENCE should be addressed to the Editor-in-Chief, Paul R. Brandon, University of Hawai'i at Mānoa, 1776 University Avenue, Castle Memorial Hall Rm 118, Honolulu, HI 96822-2463.

www.josseybass.com

Editorial Policy and Procedures

New Directions for Evaluation, a quarterly sourcebook, is an official publication of the American Evaluation Association. The journal publishes works on all aspects of evaluation, with an emphasis on presenting timely and thoughtful reflections on leading-edge issues of evaluation theory, practice, methods, the profession, and the organizational, cultural, and societal context within which evaluation occurs. Each issue of the journal is devoted to a single topic, with contributions solicited, organized, reviewed, and edited by one or more guest editors.

The editor-in-chief is seeking proposals for journal issues from around the globe about topics new to the journal (although topics discussed in the past can be revisited). A diversity of perspectives and creative bridges between evaluation and other disciplines, as well as chapters reporting original empirical research on evaluation, are encouraged. A wide range of topics and substantive domains is appropriate for publication, including evaluative endeavors other than program evaluation; however, the proposed topic must be of interest to a broad evaluation audience. For examples of the types of topics that have been successfully proposed, go to http://www.josseybass.com/WileyCDA/Section/id-155510.html.

Journal issues may take any of several forms. Typically they are presented as a series of related chapters, but they might also be presented as a debate; an account, with critique and commentary, of an exemplary evaluation; a feature-length article followed by brief critical commentaries; or perhaps another form proposed by guest editors.

Submitted proposals must follow the format found via the Association's website at http://www.eval.org/Publications/NDE.asp. Proposals are sent to members of the journal's Editorial Advisory Board and to relevant substantive experts for single-blind peer review. The process may result in acceptance, a recommendation to revise and resubmit, or rejection. The journal does not consider or publish unsolicited single manuscripts.

Before submitting proposals, all parties are asked to contact the editor-in-chief, who is committed to working constructively with potential guest editors to help them develop acceptable proposals. For additional information about the journal, see the "Statement of the Editor-in-Chief" in the Spring 2013 issue (No. 137).

Paul R. Brandon, Editor-in-Chief
University of Hawai'i at Mānoa
College of Education
1776 University Avenue
Castle Memorial Hall, Rm. 118
Honolulu, HI 96822–2463
e-mail: nde@eval.org

CONTENTS

EDITOR-IN-CHIEF'S COMMENT

Welcome to the first of two issues of *New Directions for Evaluation* on the topic of data visualization. I am sure that many readers will agree that Guest Editors Tarek Azzam and Stephanie Evergreen and their chapter authors have compiled a compelling collection of chapters, including many figures showing the novel ways that evaluation results and statistics can be displayed effectively and attractively.

When it became apparent during the production process that the large number of figures—essential parts of the chapters—made it impossible to present all the chapters in a single journal issue, the Guest Editors, the Wiley Editor, and I agreed to split the issue into two parts. (Eager future Guest Editors should note, however, that this is not meant as a precedent for future issues!)

Paul R. Brandon, PhD
Professor of Education
Curriculum Research & Development Group
College of Education
University of Hawai'i at Mānoa
Honolulu

NEW DIRECTIONS FOR EVALUATION, no. 139, Fall 2013 © Wiley Periodicals, Inc., and the American Evaluation Association. Published online in Wiley Online Library (wileyonlinelibrary.com) • DOI: 10.1002/ev.20063

EDITORS' NOTES

At the core of our profession is the need to communicate complex ideas to an array of stakeholders who may vary in their level of knowledge, interest, and familiarity with the evaluand and methods of measuring it. Data visualization offers us the ability to view data in different ways and gives us a better chance of detecting obscured patterns and connections. If designed in an appropriate way, visualizations also enable us to communicate with a myriad of stakeholders and engage them in a process of learning and discussion that can bring meaning and relevance to the data. In essence, many concepts discussed in the chapters are applicable to almost any evaluation conducted because they require evaluators to deeply understand data while pushing them to consider the underlying knowledge that can be extracted from a data set and how to best share that knowledge with others.

These topics and issues are discussed across two journal issues that deal with data visualization and evaluation. Part 1, the present issue, aims to offer a broad overview of qualitative and quantitative data visualization along with a discussion of its history, role in evaluation practice, and future trends in the area. Part 1 also includes a toolography chapter that introduces evaluators to various data visualization tools and provides a description of their main strengths and limitations. Part 2 will focus on specific applications of data visualization in evaluation that include the design and creation of data dashboards, the use of graphic recording, and the mapping of data using Geographic Information Systems (GIS). Part 2 will also contain a detailed discussion of best practices in data visualization along with multiple tips and suggestions. All chapters will examine the data visualization process from multiple perspectives and will target different ability levels.

Tarek Azzam: Editing this volume has been a real learning experience and I could not have done it without the help and support of two wonderful graduate students, Elena Harman and Molly Rottapel. I also wanted to thank Susan Kistler for initially bringing us together at AEA around this topic and Stephanie Evergreen for her tireless encouragement. Lastly, I want to thank my wife, Devon, for her eternal patience and constant support; I literally would not be able to do this without her.
Stephanie Evergreen: My thanks go to Tarek Azzam and Susan Kistler for recognizing it was prime time for this volume and to my brother, Chris Higdon, who repaired my broken but necessary *e* key at a critical moment in this volume's production.

Figure 1. Title Icons

Understanding

Collecting

Analyzing

Communicating

The beginning of each chapter contains icons (designed by Chris Metzner, see Figure 1) that indicate the applicability of the chapter to the four stages of the evaluation life cycle (Alkin, 2010). These stages include (1) understanding the program, stakeholders, and context; (2) collecting data and information; (3) analyzing data; and (4) communicating findings. These icons provide a quick reference of each chapter's content and its relationship to evaluation practice.

Part 1 Chapter Descriptions

Throughout this issue we introduce the evaluation community to recent developments in the data visualization field and offer cautions and advice for the optimal use of visualizations in evaluation practice. Chapter 1 is a broad introduction to data visualization that includes a working definition and historical roots, and includes a discussion of the role that visualization plays in evaluation practice. This chapter also provides some predictions of the future trends of data visualization and how it may impact evaluation practice, along with challenges that accompany data visualization. Chapter 2 focuses on recent developments in quantitative data visualization that range from the simple to the complex. Developments in qualitative visualization will also be addressed, beginning with Chapter 3. In this chapter readers are introduced to methods for displaying individual words, sentences, and themes, along with a discussion of the strengths and limitations of utilizing nontext or visual media to represent qualitative information. At the end of this issue, readers are presented with a toolography (Chapter 4) containing additional information on data visualization tools and software, along with a brief description and our assessment of the major advantages and drawbacks of each featured product. In all cases, the figures in each chapter have been printed in black and white; color versions can be found at www.ndedataviz.com

Reference

Alkin, M. C. (2010). *Evaluation essentials: From A to Z*. New York, NY: Guilford Press.

Tarek Azzam
Stephanie Evergreen
Editors

TAREK AZZAM is an assistant professor at Claremont Graduate University, and associate director of the Claremont Evaluation Center. His research focuses on developing new methods that attempt to address the logistical, political, and technical challenges that evaluators commonly face in practice, with the aim of improving the rigor and credibility of evaluations and increasing evaluation's potential impact on programs and policies.

STEPHANIE EVERGREEN is an evaluator who runs Evergreen Data, a data presentation consulting firm.

Azzam, T., Evergreen, S., Germuth, A. A., & Kistler, S. J. (2013). Data visualization and evaluation. In T. Azzam & S. Evergreen (Eds.), *Data visualization, part 1. New Directions for Evaluation, 139,* 7–32.

1

Data Visualization and Evaluation

Tarek Azzam, Stephanie Evergreen, Amy A. Germuth, Susan J. Kistler

Abstract

This chapter elaborates on the definition of data visualization, highlights its historical development, and offers examples of how data visualization has been used in evaluations to help aid understanding, collect data and information, conduct analysis, and communicate to a variety of stakeholders. This chapter also outlines future trends in data visualization and their potential influence on evaluation practice. The chapter concludes with some of the main limitations and cautions that are associated with data visualization. © Wiley Periodicals, Inc., and the American Evaluation Association.

One of the main challenges in writing a chapter on visualization and evaluation is that data visualization is very broad in scope and can encompass anything from qualitatively based phrase nets, such as in Figure 1.1, to quantitatively derived charts, such as in Figure 1.2. There are also various visualizations that fall within this spectrum, some pushing

Note: The figures presented in this chapter can be viewed in color by accessing www .NDEdataviz.com and selecting Chapter 1.

Figure 1.1. Phrase Net Showing Common Word Connections in Shakespeare's Plays

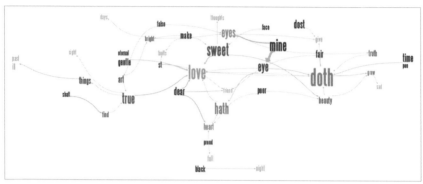

Source: Created with www.many-eyes.com

Figure 1.2. Small Multiple Display of Neighborhood Sentiment

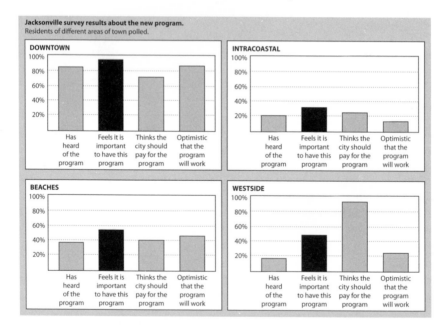

the limits of what we can visualize, and it was difficult to select from this wide variety to highlight in this chapter. During the selection process we attempted to prioritize visualizations that were new or unfamiliar to the field and that offered a meaningful contribution to the evaluation process. We were guided by the evaluation process to help us explain the value and benefit of each visualization, but were aware that the utility of a particular visualization was not limited to only one stage of evaluation, and that it could be incorporated throughout the understanding, collecting, analysis, and communication stages. This chapter was also designed to offer a breadth of understanding of the field of data visualization and its connection to evaluation by tracking its historical development, offering examples of how data visualizations are used in evaluation practice, attempting to predict future visualization trends and their effect on the field, and offering cautions that aim to reduce the potential for misuse and miscommunication. This is an ambitious task that will begin with a definition of data visualization.

What We Mean by *Data Visualization*

Our definition of data visualization relies on three criteria. Data visualization is a process that (a) is based on qualitative or quantitative data and (b) results in an image that is representative of the raw data, which is (c) readable by viewers and supports exploration, examination, and communication of the data (adapted from Kosara, 2007). Although these criteria may appear self-evident, in practice it takes thoughtful consideration and application to achieve them.

The first criterion in our definition is the simplest to achieve, because during an evaluation we often collect various forms of data that can potentially be visualized. We have purposefully kept the data criterion broad because both quantitative and qualitative data can take on many characteristics and attributes, such as is shown in Figures 1.1 and 1.2. Quantitative data can include Likert-scale items, geographic coordinates, quantified coding, various demographic characteristics, and a host of numerically based values that represent some type of information. Qualitative data are also broad in scope and can take the form of transcribed interviews, recorded conversations among stakeholders, pictures, video, or drawings that capture events, processes, and outcomes. Each of these data types requires unique approaches and methods of visualization to optimize the knowledge that they contain.

The second criterion is a reminder to examine the data carefully to ensure that the breadth and scope of the visualization does not omit important information, does not overrepresent certain data, and that the visualization accurately reflects the information contained in the data. Keeping this understanding in mind throughout the visualization development process can help to prioritize elements of visualization design so that its message reflects what is actually in the data. This criterion is also an important reminder to check for unintentional manipulation of the visualization that may lead to misunderstandings.

The final criterion of readability supporting exploration, examination, and communication can be viewed as the test of a successful visualization. Various methods for achieving this final criterion are presented in this issue, covering multiple data forms and sources. Although these methods range in scope and purpose, all require the evaluator to consider the audience and to use his or her understanding to craft a visualization that is engaging and, more importantly, enlightening. We believe that if a visualization achieves criteria 1 and 2, but fails to achieve criterion 3, then it has failed to accomplish its primary objective of helping to turn data into knowledge.

History and Current Trends in Data Visualization

Proper application and execution of these criteria in evaluation work require some understanding of the background of data visualization and how it has developed over time to include the tools we use today and the trends we anticipate in the very near future. Please note that we have created Figure 1.3 to illustrate the key historical visualizations and events that are described in the next paragraphs.

Figure 1.3. Key Historical Events in Data Visualization

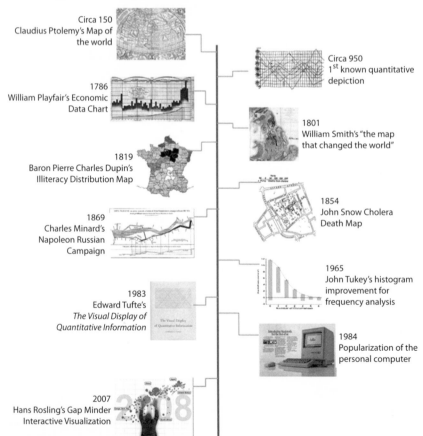

Circa 150
Claudius Ptolemy's Map of the world

Circa 950
1st known quantitative depiction

1786
William Playfair's Economic Data Chart

1801
William Smith's "the map that changed the world"

1819
Baron Pierre Charles Dupin's Illiteracy Distribution Map

1854
John Snow Cholera Death Map

1869
Charles Minard's Napoleon Russian Campaign

1965
John Tukey's histogram improvement for frequency analysis

1983
Edward Tufte's
The Visual Display of Quantitative Information

1984
Popularization of the personal computer

2007
Hans Rosling's Gap Minder Interactive Visualization

Although data visualization evolved in sister fields like survey design (Dillman, Tortora, Conradt, & Bowker, 1998), applied statistics (Bertin, 1983; Cleveland, 1993; Tukey, 1977), visual thinking, and technology and information design, the earliest seeds of visualization are found in cartography and astronomy. Early Egyptians used coordinates to lay out towns, and by 200 BC were using a lattice system similar to latitude and longitude to denote the positions of land masses and stars. In the 1st century AD, Claudius Ptolemy developed a spherical map of the earth using latitude and longitude that served as a reference standard until the 14th century (Friendly, 2009).

The first known graphical depiction of quantitative information is a circa 950 anonymous multiple time-series graph showing the changing position of the seven most prominent heavenly bodies over space and time (Friendly, 2009). However, it wasn't until the 17th century that French philosopher and mathematician Rene Descartes invented the visual representation of quantitative data in relation to two-dimensional coordinate scales. Despite these graphical innovations, William Playfair is credited as the inventor of the modern chart based on his books *Commercial and Political Atlas* (Playfair, 2005) and *Statistical Breviary* (Playfair, 2003), which displayed line and bar charts (see Figure 1.3) and pie charts, respectively, and which had the unique advantage of being widely distributed because of Gutenberg's invention of the printing press in 1450.

The early to mid-1800s saw an explosion of new data displays that pushed ideas of data representation and the social issues that they reflected, beginning with geologist William Smith's (Smith, 1815) geological map of Great Britain. Smith's representation was not only the first national-scale geological map, it was the most accurate of its time. Perhaps more critically, it depicted each local sequence of rock strata as a subsequence of a single universal sequence of strata that could be distinguished and traced for great distances by means of embedded fossilized organisms. Because this visualization provided support to the new theory of evolution and pushed ideas regarding the earth's age, many cartographers refer to it as "The Map that Changed the World" (Allen, 2010). This map also demonstrated how a visualization could be used to enhance understanding and provide factual support to contested claims.

In the 1820s Baron Charles Dupin used continuous shadings from white to black to show the distribution and degree of illiteracy in France. Titled "Carte de la France obscure et de la France éclairée" (Dupin, 1826), it attracted wide attention and may represent the first application of graphics in the social realm. It could be considered a very early attempt at visual representation of community needs. In 1855 Dr. John Snow (Snow, 1855) used a dot map to identify deaths due to cholera clustered around the infested Broad Street pump in London (Friendly, 2009), and Florence Nightingale (Nightingale, 1857) used circular area charts to show that more

British soldiers had died during the Crimean War as a result of poor hygienic conditions in battlefield hospitals than in combat. One of the most famous charts developed during this time period was Charles Minard's 1865 illustration of the decimation of Napoleon's army during the 1812 Russian campaign (Tufte, 2006).

The end of the 1800s and early 1900s saw few graphic innovations, in part due to interest in quantification and formal models. This is not to say that interest in data visualization waned. In fact, many of the data visualizations that had been developed earlier were popularized in government, commerce, and science and were used to better explain new discoveries. Willard Cope Brinton's (Brinton, 1939) publication of *Graphic Presentation* included hundreds of detailed charts, graphs, and maps, and supported this ongoing interest in data visualization, partly because it also suggested methods for improving each type of data representation. In the 1960s, John Tukey recognized the importance of visual approaches to understanding data and developed a predominantly visual approach to exploring and analyzing data called *exploratory data analysis*. By the end of that same decade Jacques Bertin published *Semilogie Graphique* (Bertin, 1967), representing the first intent to provide a theoretical foundation to information visualization, the study of interactive visual representations of abstract data to reinforce human cognition.

As use of computers became more prevalent by business and science in the 1950s and then personal computers replaced mainframes by the mid-1980s, the need to ensure computer usability by nontechnical persons supported both a focus on graphic user interfaces and the general public's ability to develop computer-based graphics. In 1984 Apple introduced the Macintosh, the first popular and affordable computer that focused on graphics. A year prior, data visualization aficionado Edward Tufte published what was to become a popular and groundbreaking book on data visualization, *The Visual Display of Quantitative Information* (Tufte, 1983). Since then, the Internet has generated a greater need for and interest in high-quality human–computer interface, and website design and research has improved our understanding of how persons perceive and understand information in charts and graphs. The development of data visualization has reached a point where individuals can directly interact with and manipulate the visualization, as was demonstrated by Rosling's (2007) TED talk, where he used bubble charts to depict life expectancy trends over time and across the globe.

Most recently we have seen the growth of data visualization tools that push information into the hands of the public and allow them to become consumers of data and to generate their own analyses. Many-eyes.com is an example of a website that allows users to upload their own data or create visualizations of available data. The Internet has forced both public and private entities to be more transparent about their work, to share their data, and to make that data available in ways that an informed citizen can make sense of it. In the United States, we've seen President Obama elevate projects like Data.gov (http://www.data.gov), the public repository of federal data. Citizens can go to County Sin Rankings at http://countysinrankings.org, a winner of the Sunlight Foundation's data visualization and access challenge, to find out about high school dropout rates, income inequality, violent crime, and other indicators within their county. Parents and educators (and anyone else) can use the Kids Count Data Center at http://datacenter.kidscount.org/ from the Annie E. Casey Foundation to rank, map, and create trend graphs for indicators of child welfare. This trend will continue as more information becomes available and the need to analyze and visualize "big data" becomes more common in society.

Current Uses of Data Visualization in Evaluation

The topic of data visualization has been of interest to the evaluation field for at least a decade and a half with the publication of a previous New Directions for Evaluation issue edited by Henry (1997) titled "Creating Effective Graphs: Solutions for a Variety of Evaluation Data," and the recent creation of the Data Visualization and Reporting Topical Interest Group (2010) within the American Evaluation Association. Given this interest and the continuing developments in data visualization software technology, processing power, and storage capacity, we believe that data visualization has reached a stage where it has become critical for the evaluation community to improve how it designs and communicates information. This was confirmed in a study by Evergreen (2011), who found that many of the visualizations used in evaluation reports tended to be confusing, potentially leading to misunderstandings and decision errors on the part of the evaluator and stakeholders. Our hope is to provide examples of interesting and effective data visualizations in this chapter and throughout the volume to help inspire and improve the relevance of data visualization in evaluation practice. In our attempt to accomplish this we have selected some innovative visualizations that can be used during different stages of the evaluation process. The following sections briefly illustrate how visualizations have been used (a) to increase our understanding of a program, its context, and history; (b) to aid in the collection of data; (c) to conduct analyses of different forms of data; and (d) to communicate to a wide range of stakeholder groups.

Understanding

During the understanding stage an evaluator is concerned with gaining insights about the program, its history, activities, stakeholders, and more generally the context in which the program operates. As evaluators begin to gather this information they can use qualitative visualization techniques, such as graphic recording, to gain insights in an interactive visual manner that encourages discussion amongst stakeholders. The graphic recording

Figure 1.4. A Photo of Graphic Recording Session in Action

approach is a facilitated group discussion that is visually represented as different topics, themes, and ideas emerge from the group (described in more detail in Part 2). Graphic recording enables the visualization of ideas and concepts that solicits stakeholders' beliefs about how their program functions and where it is located within the larger environment and community (Figure 1.4). The actual graphic recording process is as important as the final product because it allows the evaluator to gain a sense of the history and evolution of the ideas behind a program, group dynamics, and stakeholder interests and values. Graphic recording could be described as a less rigid form of program theory development or logic modeling; however, the final product is something that tells a story about a program, where it's been, where it is, and where it wants to go.

Interactive conceptual models are another approach to gaining insights about a program. Interactive conceptual models allow the evaluator to create multiple levels of understanding that begin with the broadest perspective and can end at the most detailed level. Figure 1.5 is an example of how these models could function, where the broadest level represents the overall program activities and outcomes in simple terms. When users click on an outcome they can view additional details about its scope, then click again to see the actual measures and indicators related to a specific outcome. The creation of these models is similar to a program theory development process (Donaldson, 2007); however, the evaluator can incorporate details about the outcomes, measures, and indicators while containing this information in one interactive package. This can ultimately also be used to embed data and information about the outcomes, so that the entire story of the program and its achievements can be represented visually. It is important

Figure 1.5. An Example of an Interactive Program Theory

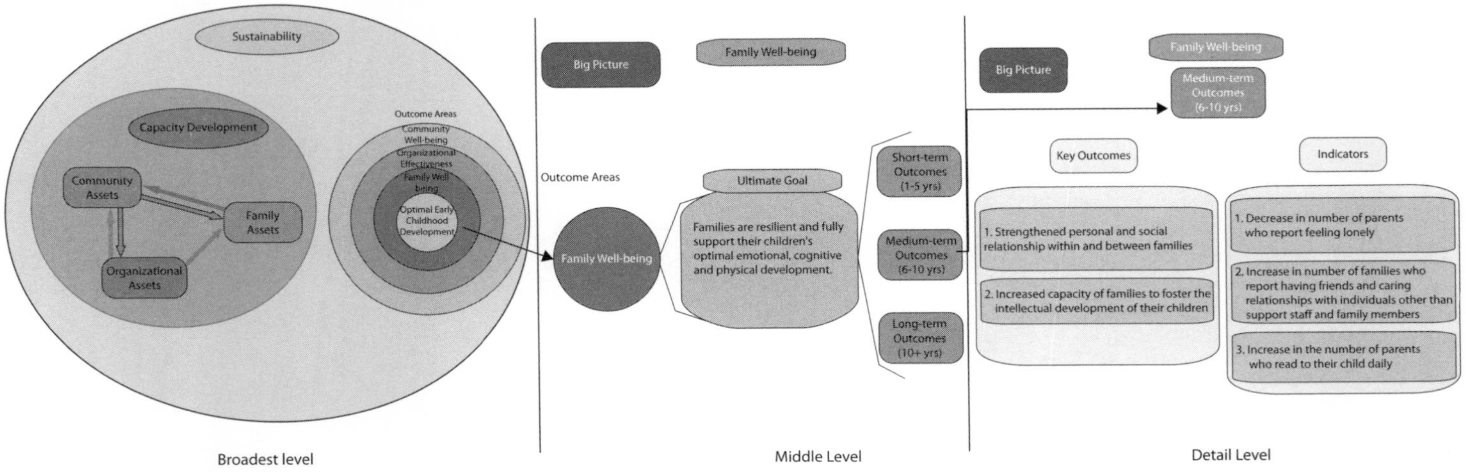

to note that this visualization does require additional technical knowledge to create, such as the use of DoView or Flash authoring software packages like Adobe Flash or Swishmax (Donaldson & Azzam, Forthcoming), but for very complex projects it is a worthwhile endeavor.

Quantitative approaches can also be used during the initial evaluation stage. For example, geographic information systems (GIS) tools (discussed in Part 2) can map the needs of the community served by a program and let an evaluation team gain a better understanding of individual and community characteristics. Figure 1.6 maps the percentage of adults who have no high school diploma (the darker the color, the larger the percentage), and also visually depicts the location of adult learning schools. Through this data visualization an evaluator can determine the level of community needs, available resources, and the potential contribution that a program can have within a specific community. This level of understanding can be gained early in the evaluation process and can significantly contribute to the development of appropriate designs and measures to inform future evaluative conclusions.

Figure 1.6. An Example of Using GIS to Conduct a Community Needs Assessment

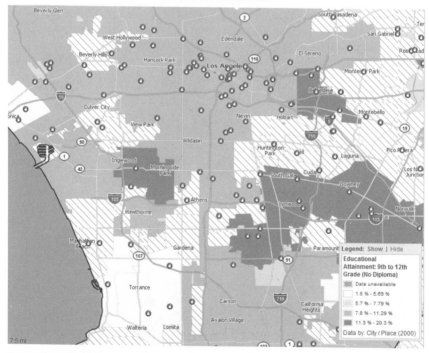

Source: Created with http://www.healthycity.org/

NEW DIRECTIONS FOR EVALUATION • DOI: 10.1002/ev

Collecting

The visual design of data collection tools and the use of collection methods that facilitate visualization have helped improve the quality of the information we gather. For example, graph enhancements like annotation and attentional cues such as arrows have garnered more credibility in evaluation because of the pioneering work of Dillman et al. (1998) in the field of survey design. Christian and Dillman (2004), for example, found that one response option was selected more often, not because it reflected respondent opinions, but because unequal spacing between response options made it stand out from the others. Additionally, they found that large text boxes for open-ended responses led to longer answers and generated more themes during analysis. Thus considerations from graphic design like position, white space, symmetry, and emphasis influence survey data collection for evaluators.

More directly, visualization has influenced data collection through methods such as adhesive formats (Fetterman & Wandersman, 2004; Paleo, 2012) or visual mapping (Stewart, 2012). In these similar methods, respondents use adhesive labels or sticky dots to mark their response on a survey, allowing for data collection and visualization to occur simultaneously (Figure 1.7). These methods can be used individually or in group settings, where the advantages of focus groups and participatory evaluation can be enhanced by data visualization that occurs during data collection. This visualization method produces instant responses that offer stakeholders a quick sense of where their group stands on issues and can help guide the focus of future data collection efforts. This is also similar to the impact of the presence of a graphic recorder in the room during a meeting in that group-based data collection using visual methods gives room for respondents to react and supports richer discussion.

Figure 1.7. An Example of Using Adhesive Formats for Data Collection

Source: www.davidfetterman.com

Analyzing

Evaluators often collect information from surveys, interviews, focus groups, databases, pictures, videos, and a myriad of other sources. Frequently this information is reduced to a single numerical value, such as a mean score, or to snippets of quotes used to convey conclusions about a program's effectiveness. Whereas these approaches remain relevant and important to our field, during the analysis stage the evaluator needs to access details visually, connect different pieces of information, identify interesting deviations and patterns, and explore information from multiple perspectives or levels. Doing so enhances the evaluator's grasp of the data, including their strengths and limitations, and allows the evaluator to detect outliers that may warn of inconsistencies in how the data were entered or point to unexpected effects of the program on a particular subgroup.

Qualitative approaches can be used to visualize main themes and capture specific ideas. Word trees and phrase nets (described in more detail in Chapter 3) provide the evaluator with the ability to see connections between ideas and concepts as they are discussed in qualitative transcripts (Figures 1.1 and Figure 1.8). Figure 1.8, for example, is a phrase tree created with the

Figure 1.8. An Interactive Phrase Tree Representing the Use of the Word *god* in the Bible

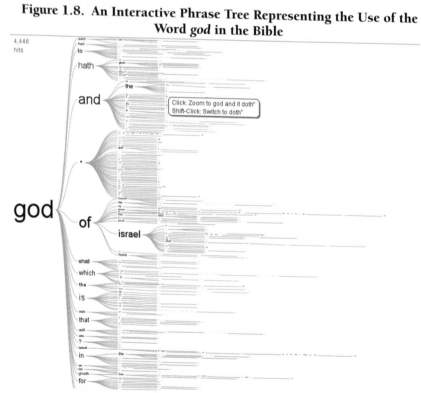

Source: Created with www.many-eyes.com

NEW DIRECTIONS FOR EVALUATION • DOI: 10.1002/ev

use of IBM's Many-eyes.com website and depicts the use of the word *god* within the Bible. As users click on each subsentence they can instantly view the full sentence and its source. This method can be helpful in the analysis of an interview transcript, as an evaluator can type in the name of the program and get a quick representation of how that program was described throughout the transcripts and the sentences within which the program name appeared. This supports pattern detection and has an added advantage of being visually engaging to stakeholders. As such, it can be used to generate discussion about findings and their potential meaning and implications.

Many of the quantitative visual analysis methods and tools (described in more detail in Chapter 2) share a common strength: the ability to dig deeper into the numbers while retaining access to a bird's-eye view of the data. The visualization process enables evaluators to detect patterns that may have remained unnoticed through other traditional methods. Many of the visualization analysis tools have been developed to serve the for-profit business sector, but their capabilities are applicable to the data analysis needs of evaluators. Currently there are software packages like Tableau, Spotfire, and SAS's J.M.P. that provide the evaluator with the power to create multiple interactive visualizations that can be used to highlight specific variables, drill down into subgroups, change the timeline, embed maps, and a host of other features. Figure 1.9 is an example of a data analysis screen that is created by Tableau that the user can directly interact with by clicking on any of the pieces of information to filter results, highlight trends, select individual cases, and change parameters. These abilities represent an important step in helping us understand the embedded knowledge that is contained in quantitative data.

Additionally, quantitative dashboards (described in more detail in Part 2) can be used to create a visual representation of how a program is performing on multiple indicators at once. These dashboards can be viewed as a way to track program performance by centralizing critical performance measures into a single visual structure. Dashboards can be designed to show whether a program is meeting its implementation quality targets, achieving performance outcomes, or is on the correct trajectory to accomplishing its goals. Figure 1.10 is an example of an operational dashboard that can be used to track implementation of different activities throughout an organization. This dashboard is designed to show trends across time, warnings if things are not working as expected, progress toward achieving goals, and a host of other critical information needed to help understand the operational effectiveness of an organization.

Other visualization methods can help answer questions about the social interactions and dynamics present between individuals and organizations. The study of social networks has been around in the social sciences since the early 1980s (Wasserman & Galaskiewicz, 1994); however, the ability to map social networks to create a visualization has become easier with developments

Figure 1.9. An Interactive Visual Tool for Analyzing Survey Data

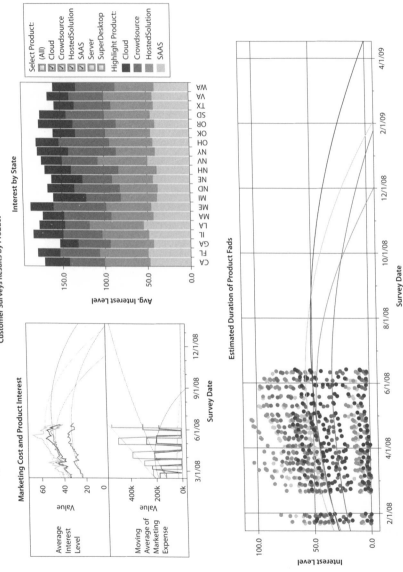

Source: Created with www.tableausoftware.com/

Figure 1.10. Dashboard for Program Implementation and Outcomes

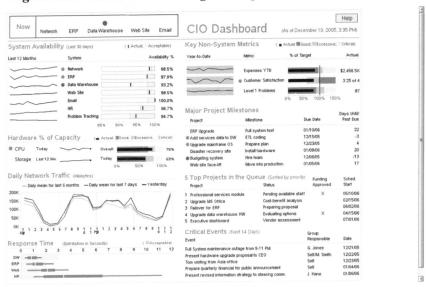

Source: Few (2006).

in software. For example, Figure 1.11 is a network map that shows how social network analysis is connected to other disciplines that are also concerned with mapping networks. This figure was created with the use of Many-eyes.com, which is a publicly available data visualization website that allows users to create these network maps and interact with the connections to highlight specific patterns or relationships.

For evaluation, social network analysis has also been used as part of the evaluation process (Fredericks & Durland, 2005), as was done in Figure 1.12, where the authors used this technique to illustrate an egocentric network with the software Netdraw in UCINET. The analysis aimed to examine the social reach of advisory board members, and this particular diagram shows one advisory board member's network. The advisory board member is represented by the darker, larger square in the center of the diagram.

Communicating

Data visualizations can also play a critical role when it is time to disseminate and communicate evaluation findings. Data visualization engages and supports program stakeholders by increasing their capacity to understand data and participate in the evaluation process. Collaboratively developed mind maps, logic models, and graphic illustrations can facilitate understanding of the findings and their implications by depicting a program's most important activities, outcomes, and ultimate goal in a concise and

Figure 1.11. A Social Network Map Showing the Connections Between Social Network Analysis and Other Disciplines

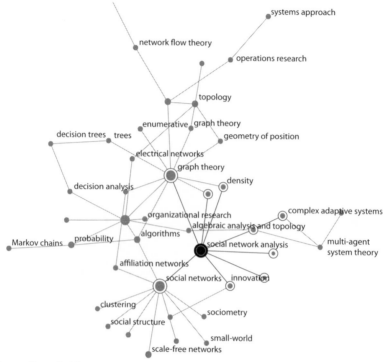

Source: Created with www.many-eyes.com

Figure 1.12. Social Network Analysis Diagram Showing the Social Reach of a Single Advisory Board Network

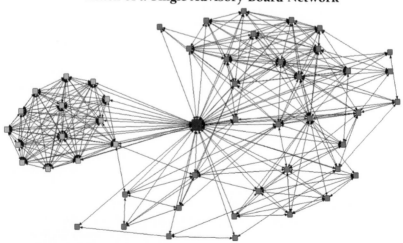

Source: Contributed by Kimberly Fredericks.

Figure 1.13. An Example of an Effectively Designed Logic Model that Is Used to Communicate to Different Stakeholders

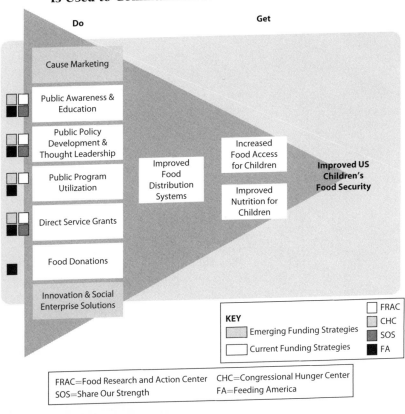

Source: Contributed by Lisa Wyatt Knowlton and Cynthia Phillips.

clear manner (Figure 1.13). Well-designed interactive visualizations for reporting and community engagement help stakeholders answer questions of import within context and place engaged stakeholders in the driver's seat in terms of defining variables and interpreting results (Knowlton & Phillips, 2012).

In addition to more traditional reporting, where data visualization elaborates narrative prose, newer methods are beginning to emerge among evaluators. For example, systems thinking has borne the visualization of causal loop diagrams as a way to depict the nuanced relationships within complex systems (Figure 1.14). The arrows in Figure 1.14 indicate the directionality of relationships among actors in the system, where in this example an increase in Demand for Power causes an increase in Electricity Generation. Pluses and minuses signal the type of relationship between the variable at the tail of the arrow and the variable at the head of the arrow. Thus

Figure 1.14. A Visualization Depicting the Directionality of Relationships Among Actors in a System

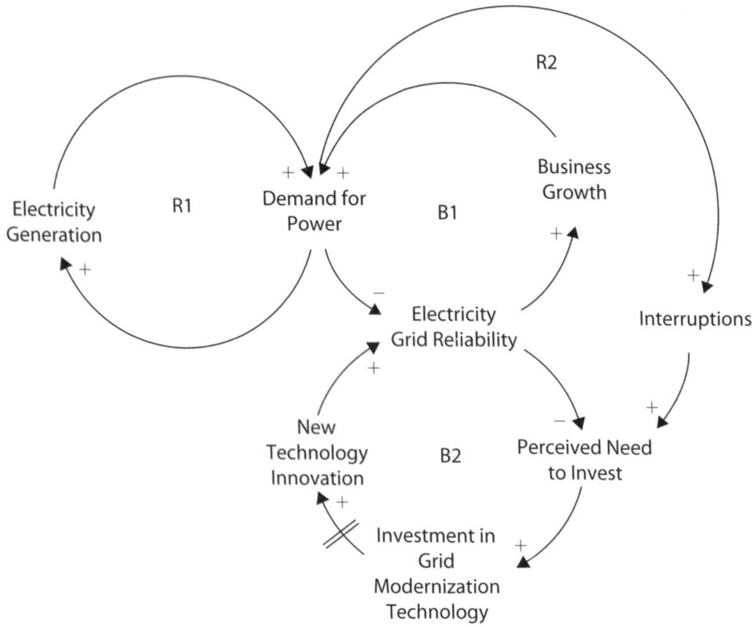

Source: Contributed by Jeff Wasbes.

the plus by Demand for Power indicates that an increase in the availability of electricity will spur increased demand; or conversely that a decrease in the availability of electricity will spur conservative behaviors and decreased demand.

Infographics are another form of data visualization becoming more popular in evaluation. Infographics are typically communication tools composed of several graphs, diagrams, or illustrations related to a single topic one page (or webpage) long. They are like dashboards in their simplicity and reliance on clear data visualizations for at-a-glance comprehension. Unlike dashboards, infographics are developed primarily for communication with external stakeholders, usually include other graphic elements like icons and typography, and sometimes coordinate the multiple graphs to tell a story about an organization. For example, Figure 1.15 provides results from a survey of nonprofits that highlights their employment trends and issues with retention, leadership, and recruitment.

Together, the examples in this section spotlight some of the ways evaluators are currently using data visualization in each phase of evaluation work.

Figure 1.15. The 2013 National Nonprofit Employment Trends Survey™ Was Produced by Nonprofit HR and Analyzed by The Improve Group

NonprofitHR.com

@nonprofit_hr | #nonprofitHRtrends

Nonprofit Employment Trends Survey (2013)

Snapshot of Current Employment Practices & Economic Trends

Nonprofits are planning for growth.

Staff Size Change (2012)

- 40% Increased
- 40% Stayed Same
- 20% Decreased

Top Growth Areas
1. Direct Services
2. Program Management/Support
3. Fundraising/Development

Plan to Create Staff Positions

100%

- 34% (2011)
- 43% (2012)
- 44% (2013)

0%

Only 7% plan to eliminate staff (2013)

87% of nonprofits surveyed believe **turnover rates will remain steady** (around 17%)

69% of nonprofits are NOT prepared for leadership succession.

As the baby boom generation of nonprofit leaders retire, the lack of a formal succession plan may endanger nonprofits' ability to effectively prepare for leadership transition and **put organizational sustainability at risk.**

9 out of 10

lack formal retention strategies.

Top areas experiencing retention challenge are the SAME as top growth areas.

Nonprofits continue to struggle with workforce diversity and inclusion.

Greatest Challenges

- Retaining staff under the age of 30 — 38%
- Staff reflecting the composition of the communities they serve — 32%
- Balancing ethnic and cultural diversity — 26%

0% ——— 100%

Social networking sites continue to grow in popularity as recruitment tools in the nonprofit sector.

Survey data show that formal and informal networking currently remain the most popular and effective recruiting methods of nonprofits, but the use of social networking sites—in particular LinkedIn and Facebook—is growing rapidly.

% Increase in Use *for Recruitment*
(in comparison to previous year's responses)

30% Facebook *(4 out of 10 use)*

25% LinkedIn *(5 out of 10 use)*

New hiring practices indicate an effort by nonprofits to avoid employee burnout.

% Hiring New Staff

100%
- 29% (2010)
- 37% (2013)
0%

% Using Current Staff

100%
- 57% (2010)
- 48% (2013)
0%

...to support new programs or initiatives

The 2013 national Nonprofit Employment Trends Survey™ has been produced annually by Nonprofit HR since 2007. 2013 Survey includes responses from more than 550 nonprofits nationwide. View the complete report online at: NonprofitHR.com. Survey and analysis by The Improve Group. Infographic design by Visual Voice.

Nonprofit **HR Solutions**

Note: Infographic Design by Elissa Schloesser at Visual Voice.

Future Trends and Challenges

Understanding the development of data visualization within and outside the field of evaluation is important for giving us a perspective on its past history and where we might go in the future. We anticipate three future trends and four closely related challenges that will likely shape the way evaluators adopt and use data visualization practices. Because these trends and challenges will likely coalesce to heighten expectations for how evaluators analyze and report data, as a community we should strive to remain near or at the cutting edge of these changes.

Development in data visualization has seen exponential growth in the past few years. This is partly due to increased interest in data about our lives and culture, increased availability of online sources for data and visualization, and increased interactivity that has emerged through the introduction of technology like the iPad and Windows 8. We believe that these developments will continue and that the trend will be toward the active engagement of stakeholders in the visualization process and the need for evaluators to facilitate this engagement. We foresee that stakeholders will become more accustomed to interpreting, creating, and interacting with data visualizations. They may come to expect visualizations containing multiple perspectives on their programs and may require evaluators to produce such products as part of the evaluation. Advances in visualization software applications have become available for public consumption and use, often at no financial expense. For example, programs like ManyEyes, Tableau Public, and Gapminder now provide Web-based services that let users upload data for custom visualizations, allowing them to analyze and interact with the information at their own pace and with their own focus.

This trend, when adopted by stakeholders, may require us to be more transparent about the data we collect, as demand for raw data increases. This particular prediction about transparency is already becoming a reality in the government sector, where the United States has funded and established data.gov, which aims to create a comprehensive repository of data that can be accessed, downloaded, and analyzed by any concerned citizen interested in issues that range from health care to environmental policy. The United Nations has also supported this trend by releasing large databases (http://data.un.org/) to help increase access and transparency, driven by their desire to be more open and accountable as well as the need to make sense of large amounts of information. Transparency has become more urgent as funding has tightened and the need for accountability increased. As such, data sharing is viewed as one approach to involve the public and show them the work being done by organizations. The second motivator for this trend is the need to understand what the data are saying. Many organizations collect large quantities of data without the capacity to analyze all of it. The hope is that members of the public will use these data to conduct their own analysis and generate knowledge that would otherwise be missed if the data remained cloistered. We believe that this trend will be a strong driver of future data policies and will lead to increased demands on openness of the data we collect.

Interactivity is also part of this trend, and we believe that it will increase in future importance. If data visualizations are designed to draw attention, software will need to incorporate methods to keep that attention. The ability to drill down into data and customize reporting appears to be the next step in data visualization. For example, when a client hovers on a peak data point, he or she should be one click away from seeing that data disaggregated by subgroups. Some software programs, Tableau, Spotfire, and SAS's J.M.P., for example, already allow such visualization. However, the learning curve for manipulating new software programs can be steep and expensive. In the struggle between familiarity and customizability, we believe the most useful data displays will be those that include both characteristics.

Challenges

Evaluators and end users of data visualizations should also bear in mind what data visualization cannot do. There are several limitations or cautions to be considered when employing data visualization techniques. The first limitation of data displays concerns issues related to causality. One of the main purposes of data visualization is to illustrate relationships pointedly. However, visualizations can easily mislead readers into thinking that relationships or patterns exist when in reality they do not. If seeing is believing, then visualizing data can exacerbate the fallacies perpetuated by questionable statistics such as spurious correlations (Figure 1.16).

Relatedly, the second caution we heed in developing data displays is the reliability of data and information. The foundation of any visualization is the data used to create it. Visualizations can actually highlight the garbage in–garbage out problem. If data contain issues such as missing values, unrepresentative samples, or other problems, then it is the evaluator's responsibility to acknowledge those limitations clearly through the use of footnotes or other indicators to avoid misleading stakeholders. Although lengthier narrative reporting can more easily integrate caveats, explanations of confidence levels, and declarations of significance levels, such important statements of uncertainty are not as easily rendered in a data visualization. As Ware (2013) noted, "The problem is that once data is [sic] represented as a visual object, it attains a kind of literal concrete quality that makes the viewer think it is accurate" (p. 28).

The third caution of data visualization is related to introducing new or unfamiliar visualizations to stakeholders. Tufte (2006) says that much of the trouble with poor graphics is due to the fact that most professional artists have little familiarity or skill with quantitative data, given that their primary study was fine art. The opposite also may be true: most researchers and evaluators have little familiarity or skill with graphic design and art. Technology has made developing visuals more accessible for those of us

NEW DIRECTIONS FOR EVALUATION • DOI: 10.1002/ev

Figure 1.16. Causation Warning

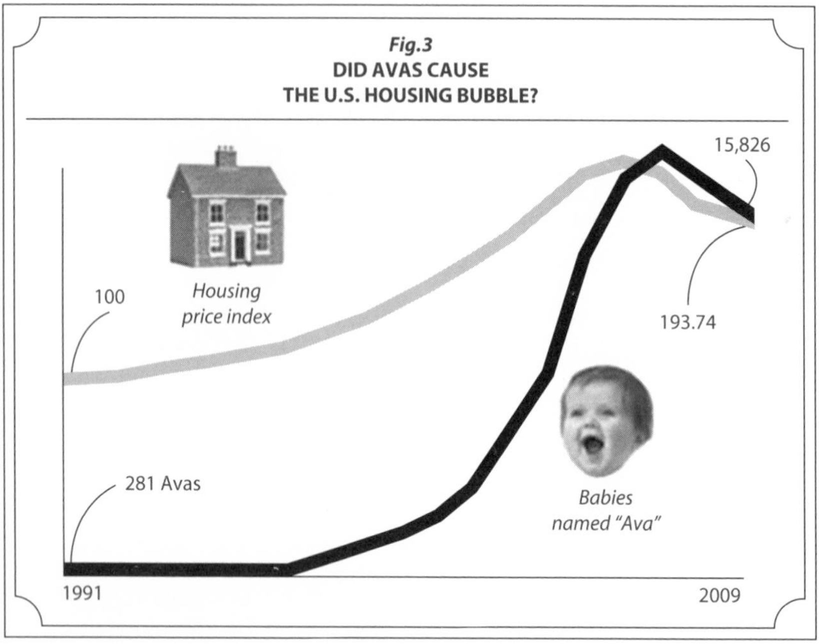

Fig.3
DID AVAS CAUSE
THE U.S. HOUSING BUBBLE?

15,826

100 *Housing price index*

193.74

281 Avas

Babies named "Ava"

1991   2009

Note: Created by Vali Chandrasekaran;
source: http://www.businessweek.com/magazine/correlation-or-causation-12012011-gfx.html

without formal graphic design or fine art training. Evaluators are wise to be thoughtful about audience frustration levels when introducing new types of graphic displays and should consider whether directly training stakeholders on display interpretation may also be needed to reduce audience frustration and misinterpretation.

The fourth limitation of our current use of data visualization is about understanding the connection between the visualization and the evaluation purpose/question. Evaluations often contain multiple data sources and analyses; however, not every analysis requires a visualization. In selecting which visualizations to create, the evaluator needs to keep in mind the main evaluation questions and design visualizations that can clearly support the answer to those questions. As we discuss in Part 2, it is important to highlight the most important information when designing visualizations so as not to obscure the most relevant evaluation findings.

Final Thoughts

Our intention in the issue is to introduce the evaluation community to visualization developments that have the potential to change or improve how we evaluate. But, as with any new idea or approach, we are likely to encounter

Figure 1.17. Depiction of the Hype Cycle

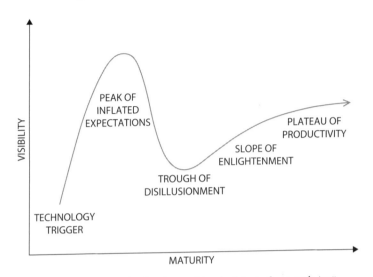

Source: http://www.gartner.com/technology/research/methodologies/hype-cycle.jsp#

setbacks as we adjust to the capabilities of these new approaches. This process of learning, struggle, and development has been described in the technology arena as the Hype Cycle (Fenn & Time, 2008; Figure 1.17). The five-phase Hype Cycle begins with the *technological trigger*, when the new idea or concept is introduced. This is followed by mass excitement and over-estimation of its relevance and benefit—the *peak of inflated expectations*. Next, as we begin to recognize the limitations associated with the technology, we enter the *trough of disillusionment*, followed by a slow but steady progression to understanding its actual potential as we climb the *slope of enlightenment*. Finally we reach the *plateau of productivity*, characterized by acceptance and wide adoption of the technology by the communities it serves.

We anticipate that some of the ideas and concepts introduced in this chapter and issue will follow the Hype Cycle trajectory, beginning with increased expectations as the tools and approaches are implemented across various evaluation projects and with multiple evaluation stakeholders that may or may not be well suited. As time progresses, the limitations and drawbacks of different visualizations will become more apparent and heightened expectations will become more tempered. Ultimately we believe that our community will progress along the slope of enlightenment and move toward the plateau of productivity. During these last two stages, the appropriate use of visualizations in evaluation will become more evident, many of the limitations will be acknowledged, and some may even be solved. The key is to remain focused on the core purposes for creating a visualization, which are to offer stakeholders an opportunity to explore, reflect, and generate knowledge from the data collected during the evaluation process.

By the time this manuscript is published, important new data visualization software packages and techniques will be on the market and some of the ones we have mentioned here will be out of business or, worse, passé. Regardless of the rise or fall of specific visualization platforms and strategies, we believe that data visualization is here to stay. It will continue to evolve and will increasingly play a critical role in the evaluation process.

References

Allen, S. (2010, July 8). Data visualization [Blog]. Retrieved from http://interaction design.sva.edu/classes/datavisualization/2010/07/08/introduction/

Bertin, J. (1967). Sémiologie graphique: Les diagrammes, les réseaux, les cartes [Graphic semiology: Diagrams, networks, maps]. Paris, France: Gauthier-Villars.

Bertin, J. (1983). Semiology of graphics: Diagrams, networks, maps. Madison, WI: The University of Wisconsin Press.

Brinton, W. C. (1939). Graphic presentation. New York, NY: Brinton Associates.

Christian, L. M., & Dillman, D. A. (2004). The influence of graphical and symbolic language manipulations on responses to self-administered questions. Public Opinion Quarterly, 68(1), 57–80.

Cleveland, W. S. (1993). A model for studying display methods of statistical graphics. Journal of Computational and Graphical Statistics, 2(4), 323–343.

Dillman, D. A., Tortora, R. D., Conradt, J., & Bowker, D. K. (1998, August). Influence of plain vs. fancy design on response rates for web surveys. Paper presented at the Joint Statistical Meetings, Dallas, TX. Retrieved from http://survey.sesrc.wsu.edu/dillman /papers/1998/influenceofplain.pdf

Donaldson, S. I. (2007). Program theory-driven evaluation science: Strategies and applications. Mahwah, NJ: Erlbaum.

Donaldson, S. I., & Azzam, T. (Forthcoming). Developing complex theories of change: The promise of technology-enhanced interactive conceptual frameworks.

Dupin, C. (1826). Carte figurative de l'instruction populaire de la France, Jobard [Figurative map of the population's level education in Jobard, France]. Paris, France: Bibliothèque Nationale de France.

Evergreen, S. D. H. (2011). Eval + comm. New Directions for Evaluation, 131, 41–46.

Fenn, J., & Time, M. (2008). Mastering the hype cycle: How to choose the right innovation at the right time. Boston, MA: Harvard Business Press.

Fetterman, D. M., & Wandersman, A. (Eds.). (2004). Empowerment evaluation principles in practice. New York, NY: Guilford Press.

Few, S. (2006). Information dashboard design: The effective visual communication of data. Sebastopol, CA: O'Reilly Media.

Fredericks, K. A., & Durland, M. M. (2005). The historical evolution and basic concepts of social network analysis. New Directions for Evaluation, 107, 15–23.

Friendly, M. (2009). Milestones in the history of thematic cartography, statistical graphics, and data visualization. Retrieved from http://www.math.yorku.ca/SCS/Gallery /milestone/milestone.pdf

Henry, G. (Ed.). (1997). Creating effective graphs: Solutions for a variety of evaluation data. New Directions for Evaluation, 73, 1–6.

Knowlton, L. W., & Phillips, C. C. (2012). The logic model guidebook: Better strategies for great results. Thousand Oaks, CA: Sage.

Kosara, R. (2007, July). Visualization criticism—The missing link between information visualization and art. *Information Visualization, IV'07. 11th International Conference* (pp. 631–636). doi: 10.1109/IV.2007.2

Nightingale, F. (1857). *Mortality of the British army.* London, England: Harrison and Sons.

Paleo, L. (2012, October). *Adhesive formats for data collection—Practice and validity of dots, stickers, and labels.* Paper presented at the meeting of the American Evaluation Association, Minneapolis, MN.

Playfair, W. (2003). Statistical breviary; shewing, on a principle entirely new, the resources of every state and kingdom in Europe, Wallis, London. In P. H. Rossi, H. E. Freeman, & M. W. Lipsey (Eds.), *Evaluation: A systematic approach.* Thousand Oaks, CA: Sage. (Original work published 1801)

Playfair, W. (2005). Commercial and political atlas: Representing, by copper-plate charts, the progress of the commerce, revenues, expenditure, and debts of England, during the whole of the eighteenth century. In H. Wainer & I. Spence (Eds.), *The commercial and political atlas and statistical breviary.* Cambridge, England: Cambridge University Press. (Original work published 1786)

Rosling, H. (2007, March). New insights on poverty [Video file]. Presentation at TED conference. Retrieved from http://www.ted. com/talks/lang/en/hans_rosling_reveals_new_insights_on_poverty.html

Smith, W. (1815). *A delineation of the strata of England and Wales, with part of Scotland; exhibiting the collieries and mines, the marshes and fenlands originally overflowed by the sea, and the varieties of soil according to the substrata, illustrated by the most descriptive names.* London, England: John Cary.

Snow, J. (1855). *On the mode of communication of cholera* (2nd ed.). London, England: n.p.

Stewart, B. (2012). Image grouping tool (Coffee Break Demonstration webinar no. 113) [Video file]. Fairhaven, MA: American Evaluation Association. Retrieved from http://comm.eval.org/EVAL/Resources/ViewDocument/?DocumentKey=8840ee00–933c-4624–9bb9–1bad15c03978

Tufte, E. R. (1983). *The visual display of quantitative information.* Chesire, CT: Graphics Press.

Tufte, E. R. (2006). *Beautiful evidence.* Cheshire, CT: Graphics Press.

Tukey, J. W. (1977). *Exploratory data analysis.* Reading, MA: Addison-Wesley.

Ware, C. (2013). *Information visualization: Perception for design* (3rd ed.). Waltham, MA: Morgan Kaufmann.

Wasserman, S., & Galaskiewicz, J. (Eds.). (1994). *Advances in social network analysis: Research in the social and behavioral sciences.* Thousand Oaks, CA: Sage.

TAREK AZZAM is an assistant professor at Claremont Graduate University, and associate director of the Claremont Evaluation Center. His research focuses on developing new methods that attempt to address the logistical, political, and technical challenges that evaluators commonly face in practice, with the aim of improving the rigor and credibility of evaluations and increasing evaluation's potential impact on programs and policies.

STEPHANIE EVERGREEN is an evaluator who runs Evergreen Data, a data presentation consulting firm.

AMY A. GERMUTH is an independent evaluator and owner of EvalWorks, LLC, an evaluation and survey consulting firm in Durham, NC.

SUSAN J. KISTLER is the executive director of the American Evaluation Association and the owner of iMeasureMedia. She has shepherded AEA's evolution over the past 10 years through an era of technological evolution to where it is at the forefront of associations its size in terms of the adoption and leveraging of technology and social media in pursuit of its mission and goals.

NEW DIRECTIONS FOR EVALUATION • DOI: 10.1002/ev

Lysy, C. (2013). Developments in quantitative data display and their implications for evaluation. In T. Azzam & S. Evergreen (Eds.), *Data visualization, part 1. New Directions for
Evaluation, 139*, 33–51.

2

Developments in Quantitative Data Display and Their Implications for Evaluation

Christopher Lysy

Abstract

*Quantitative displays discussed in this chapter can be used across multiple eval-
uation stages, although this chapter pays significant attention to visualization
as a mechanism for communicating data and results. The chapter is split into
two parts. The first part illustrates some newer chart types that have gained
popularity over the last decade, and identifies evaluation situations where these
new visualizations could be useful. The second part examines new display functionality made possible by the Web and discusses how these features can be used
to increase the amount of data presented while maintaining visual simplicity.*
© Wiley Periodicals, Inc., and the American Evaluation Association.

When an issue of *New Directions for Evaluation* (NDE) last tackled
the concept of data visualization 15 years ago, the authors con-
cluded the volume with some simple suggestions for improved
graphing (Henry & Dolan, 1997). These suggestions boiled down to knowing

Note: The figures presented in this chapter can be viewed in color by accessing www
.NDEdataviz.com and selecting Chapter 2.

the graph's purpose, the audience, the technology, and the presentation media while understanding one's own capabilities. From a broad perspective, little has changed. The rules governing good data visualization are the same rules that govern good communication.

Fifteen years ago graphs lived in paper reports, slides, and transparencies. The Web, still very much in a nascent form, had yet to develop into a presentation platform capable of more than just distributing these static charts to a wider audience. With static charts simplicity in form often meant simplicity in content, a point that was made clear in several chapters of Henry and Dolan (1997). For example, Bonnet notes that "the fact that it is possible to squeeze a lot of information into a graph does not necessarily make it a good idea to do so" (1997, p. 14). DeVeaux adds that "when reducing data to graphs, evaluators should strive to avoid clutter and the temptation to squeeze too much information into a limited space" (1997, p. 73). In their conclusion, Henry and Dolan continue the argument, "one common mistake in graphical design is in trying to accomplish too much with one graph by packing too much information in, so that the graph becomes unintelligible or confusing to the audience" (1997, p. 104).

Today, the Web has become more than just a mechanism for sending static visuals out to a broader audience. Instead evaluators can present large quantitative data sets without simplifying the content. By utilizing the Web as a presentation platform, evaluators can now take advantage of new features such as interactivity, animation, and automation to make large complex data sets clutter free and approachable for lay audiences. However, we should not lose sight of the importance and value of static images and their role in evaluation reporting and communication.

In an attempt to strike a balance between developments in static visualization and the new visualization opportunities that the Web has provided, this chapter will be divided into two parts. Part 1 will focus on variations of static (or traditional) charts and will include examples of new developments in this area and how they can be used in evaluation practice. Part 2 of the chapter will focus on Web-based data presentation and charting and highlight some of the latest developments in this arena. The chapter will end with some final thoughts on the state of the field and its application to evaluation practice.

Part 1. Variations on the Traditional Chart

The best chart types for displaying quantitative data are often the simplest. Bar charts, line graphs, and scatterplots are as effective today as they were 15 years ago. Many of the charts now in style are just variants of the old stalwarts. These variants can be useful, but are not major developments. So what is new? The following section identifies evolutions on traditional charts that have gained popularity over the last decade. They include sparkcharts, heat maps, bubble charts, tree maps, and stack graphs. For each of these static charts I've provided a brief description and offered an example of how it can be displayed and described.

Sparkcharts

Sparkcharts, an invention of Edward Tufte (2006), help with the visual presentation of data in small spaces. Sparkcharts are now a standard feature on Excel 2010, a change likely influenced by the popularity of Excel add-ons, like BonaVista Systems' Micro Charts (Gemignani, 2006). Sparkcharts are particularly useful for showing distributions and plotting time-series data. They can fit within a single cell in an Excel worksheet or within a line of text in a document. There are two common types of sparkcharts: sparkbars, which are simply small bar charts, and sparklines, which are simply small line graphs.

Sparkbars. Before presenting descriptive data it is always wise to visualize the overall distribution. Interesting patterns are not always noticeable by looking solely at the mean and standard deviation. Although the sparkbar feature in Excel does not allow for the bars to touch, it can be used like a histogram to add more depth to a table of descriptive statistics. Figure 2.1 includes five cases, each with an N of 25, a mean of 3.0, and a range of 1–5. By using sparkbars within Excel we can see that the overall distribution and subsequently the standard deviation vary considerably, thus alerting us to potentially interesting patterns in the data.

Sparklines. Line graphs that show more than one line can be useful for making comparisons, but sometimes it is important to discuss each individual line. By using sparklines evaluators can call attention to and discuss individual cases. Sparklines can be embedded within a sentence to illustrate a trend and help stakeholders better understand the data. Evaluators can use this simple visualization when creating reports. The

Figure 2.1. Example Table with Sparkbars, Created With the Use of Microsoft Excel 2010

N	Mean	Standard Deviation	Range	Sparkbar
25	3.0	1.4	1–5	▬ ▬ ▬ ▬ ▬
25	3.0	2.0	1–5	▮ __ ▮
25	3.0	1.7	1–5	▮ ▬ __ ▬ ▮
25	3.0	0.7	1–5	__ ▬ ▮ ▬ __
25	3.0	1.2	1–5	__ ▬ ▮ ▬

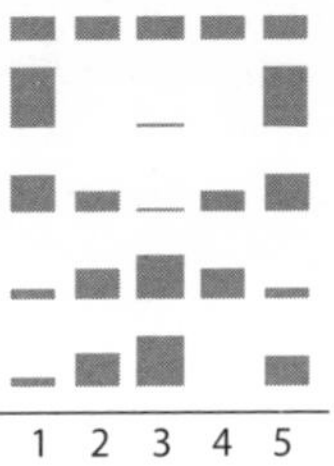

1 2 3 4 5

NEW DIRECTIONS FOR EVALUATION • DOI: 10.1002/ev

following example is a simple template of what a report might look like with sparkline inclusion, where each of the five sparklines represents 15 individual data points that range from 1 (low satisfaction) to 5 (high satisfaction):

Case number one has the lowest mean at 2.1, �—⌒⌐ but the sparkline shows a promising upward trend. Case number two has the second lowest mean at 2.3, but shows a far less promising trend ⌐⌒⌐. Case number three has a mean of 2.7 and shows another upward trend ⌐⌒⌐. Case number four has the second highest mean at 3.1, but seems to have stabilized ⌐⌒⌐. Case number five has the highest mean at 3.5, but shows what is likely the second least promising trend ⌐⌒⌐.

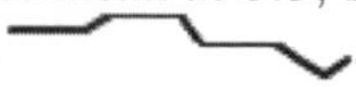

Twitter Friendly

With so many programs distributing reports on Twitter it could be useful to showcase a specific finding. With the help of ASCII characters, sparkbars can be included within the 140-character limits of Twitter (http://www .datadrivenconsulting.com/2010/06/twitter-sparkline-generator/) (Kerin, 2010). For example, the following distribution of 1, 2, 3, 4, 5, 5, 4, 3, 2, 1 can be represented in under 20 characters and is a quick and innovative way to share data trends with interested stakeholders.

▄▖▖▪▪█▌▪▪▖▖▄.

Heat Mapping

Heat mapping is a newer advance in data visualization where color is applied to various values to represent data categories to a viewer quickly and visually. This section discusses two examples of heat mapping.

Conditional formatting for reporting. During the report writing phase of an evaluation it is often important to keep certain sets of variables in a specific order throughout the report. This is especially true for long lists of states or counties, where sorting each table in different ways could make it hard to locate specific rows from table to table. The downside of keeping the tables consistent is it limits an evaluator's ability to call attention to numbers falling above or below certain thresholds.

Heat mapping is essentially using conditional formatting, often color, to focus a reader's attention on specific data points. Evaluators can use different colors to highlight whether output measures were met and different gradients of a single color to provide a sense of range.

In Figure 2.2, I have highlighted any cell that shows an infant death rate (per 1,000 births) higher than 9.1 in dark gray. In a second color I have

**Figure 2.2. Example Heat Map Table, Created with the Use of
Microsoft Excel 2010**

County	2010 Infant Deaths	2010 Rate	2011 Infant Deaths	2011 Rate
County 1	12	6.5	11	6.6
County 2	2	5.2	2	6.3
County 3	1	10	0	0
County 4	0	0	1	3.5
County 5	1	3.7	0	0
County 6	3	17.3	3	21.1
County 7	6	10.9	3	6.1
County 8	3	15.1	0	0
County 9	2	5.4	3	8.8
County 10	4	3.8	8	7.6
County 11	16	6.2	13	5.1
County 12	6	6.9	7	8.1

highlighted any cell that shows an infant death rate (per 1,000 births) between 7.41 and 9.1 in light gray. By using these colors I was able to call attention to the specific cells easily, without needing to re-sort and break up the order of the table.

Conditional formatting for data cleaning. Microsoft Excel and other spreadsheet programs are like the Swiss Army knives of data programs. Spreadsheets are used to enter, sort, filter, combine, analyze, visualize, and occasionally collect quantitative data. Also, just about every Web survey program exports into a spreadsheet-friendly format by default. But spreadsheets have an Achilles' heel. Whether it is an accidental backspace that clears out a cell, a bad sort or filter that fails to highlight all the necessary columns, or a copy and paste that holds onto a little more data than necessary, data in spreadsheets are easy to corrupt.

One way to assist with data cleaning is to use conditional formatting to create heat maps within your data table. When looking at large data sets, and sometimes even small data sets, it can be easy to miss bad data. By setting up conditional formatting with noticeable colors to pinpoint duplicate IDs or out-of-range values, an analyst can better catch potential issues.

Conditions can be set on entire worksheets, individual columns, groups of cells, or even a single cell. In the example in Figure 2.3, I have set conditional formatting rules to highlight any duplicate ID numbers. I have also used the formatting to highlight blank cells, cells with negative values, and cells containing specific text. The specialty formatting will only show

Figure 2.3. Example Data Sheet With Conditional Formatting, Created With the Use of Microsoft Excel 2010

ID	Q1	Q2	Q3	Q4	Q5	Q6
1053	1	2	−9		1	2
1054	2	2	4	6	1	
1055	1	1	3	1	2	5
1055	2	1	9	1	1	6
1057	3	2	7	3	1	1
1058	3	1	L	2	2	2
1059	4	1	4	4	1	2
1060	1	2	3	2	1	3
1061	2	1	5	3	2	4
1061	1	1	4	1	1	6
1063	4	2	6	1	1	

if the conditions are met and will exist passively within a sheet unless it is cleared. So if in the above example a number is accidentally erased, the cell will immediately become highlighted. When a number is entered into a highlighted cell, the highlight will disappear. This formatting option is available in Excel (and accessed through the Help menu) and can serve as a powerful aid during data cleaning and organization.

Bubble Chart

Scatterplots are still the go-to visualization when one is examining relationships between continuous variables. One of the problems with the traditional scatterplot is that all data points are presented as if they are on equal footing. There are many times when they are not, like a county with a population of 800,000 appearing as a scatterplot point sized the same as a county of 30,000.

Bubble maps are scatterplots with added dimensions. The most common usage is to add weight to individual data points based on population. A school with 1,000 kids would produce a bubble 10 times larger than a school with 100 kids. In order to keep larger bubbles from obscuring smaller bubbles, they are often designed with a certain level of transparency. Color can also be used as an additional feature to code categorical data.

In the fictitious example below (Figure 2.4), schools in a district are plotted using average household income on the y-axis and average test score on the x-axis. Shading is used to show which are elementary schools, middle schools, or high schools. Bubble size is determined by the student population in each school. Bubble charts can be created with the use of Excel 2010.

Figure 2.4. Example Bubble Chart, Created With the Use of Google Spreadsheet

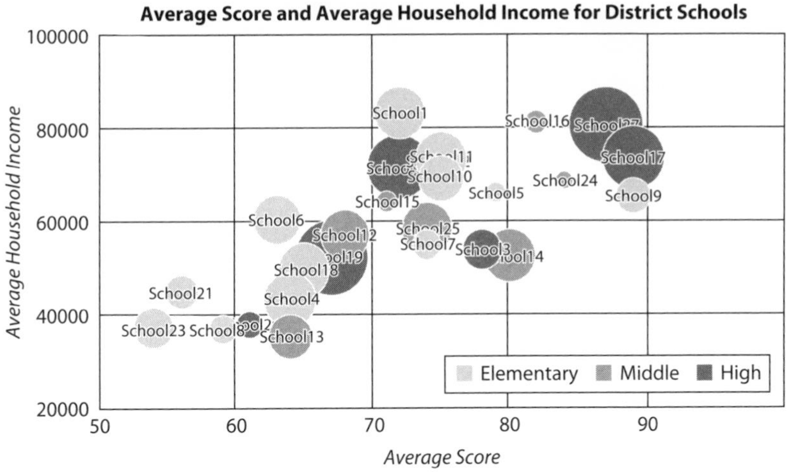
Average Score and Average Household Income for District Schools
100000
80000
60000
40000
20000
Average Household Income
50
60
70
80
90
Average Score
Elementary
Middle
High
School1
School16
School17
School10
School24
School5
School9
School15
School6
School12
School25
School7
School3
School18
School21
School4
School23
School8
School13

Tree Map

There are times when evaluators want to show the breakdown of a budget or some other whole that can be dispersed into parts. Pie charts have often been used for this purpose in the past but they can quickly become confusing with more than a few slices. Pie charts have also fallen out favor and their usage can generate debate. For a taste of the argument against pie charts, read the Gargani (2012) blog post "Should the Pie Chart Be Retired?"

Tree maps are similar to pie charts in that they show parts of a whole but, unlike pie charts, they can incorporate more individual pieces without cluttering the graphic. Tree maps are particularly good at presenting information like budgets, which often include more elements than can be effectively communicated through a pie chart.

The following example uses a simple budget (Table 2.1). I have created a pie chart just to give an example of how these data look in pie chart form (Figure 2.5). Following the pie chart is an example tree map that uses both color and size to show the distribution of funds in a budget (Figure 2.6). Because data are most often presented in a rectangular format (i.e., paper, computer screens, PowerPoint slides) the visual is able to fill up the landscape. Smaller blocks that would usually disappear in a pie chart can be seen with relative ease. The ability to create tree maps can be installed as an add-on to Microsoft Excel by downloading the Microsoft Treemapper application.

Stack Graph

We use line graphs when we want to visualize how a variable changes over time. We may also be interested in knowing about the way the time-series variable breaks down. For example, an evaluator may want to look at the

Table 2.1. **Example Budget Table for Tree Map**

Department	Budget
Fundraising	15,000
Marketing	50,000
Evaluation	10,000
Program	150,000
Information technology	50,000
Human resources	60,000
Outreach	10,000

**Figure 2.5. Example Pie Chart,
Created With the Use of
Microsoft Excel 2010**

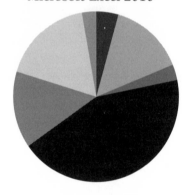

- ■ Fundraising   ■ Information Technology
- ■ Marketing   ■ Human Resources
- ■ Evaluation   ■ Outreach
- ■ Program

change in population over time but also needs to understand how that population breaks down by ethnicity. He or she could visualize with a single line graph for the broad trend and a series of pie charts for each ethnicity, but it would take up too much real estate, and some important contextual information would be lost.

To address this issue an evaluator can use stack graphs, also known as area charts, which are used to chart how a specific variable breaks down over time. Instead of beginning at the x-axis, visuals for each subcomponent start where the previous component stopped. In essence, the subvariables are stacked on top of each other, making it possible to see the overall total trend and the change in the individual components.

New Directions for Evaluation • DOI: 10.1002/ev

Figure 2.6. Example Tree Map, Created With the Use of IBM ManyEyes

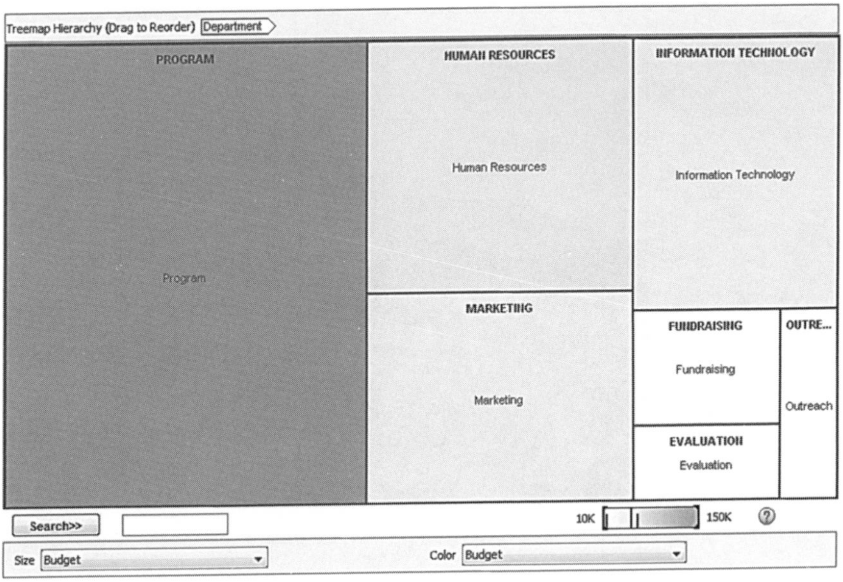

The fictional example shown in Figure 2.7 depicts the growth of a population over several decades. The population variable is then broken down by language.

Part 2: The Web and New Display Features

The following section identifies three new quantitative display features made possible by the Web: interactivity, animation, and automation. For each one of these possibilities I offer an example or two to highlight their available features and potential use in evaluation practice. Finally, I discuss some of the concerns that accompany the new features.

Interactive Data Display Systems

In order to avoid clutter when creating static data visualizations, evaluators are usually forced to limit the amount of data shown. Data that may have the highest relevance for any individual stakeholder or report reader is often far too detailed to appear in most reports. Statewide average test scores can be somewhat interesting, but many parents want to know what is happening in their own school and how that compares to surrounding schools. Crime rates citywide may be on the rise but what is happening in a specific neighborhood, on a specific street corner? Interactive data visualization not only allows evaluators to provide a general overview but

Figure 2.7. Example Stack Graph, Created With the Use of Microsoft Excel 2010

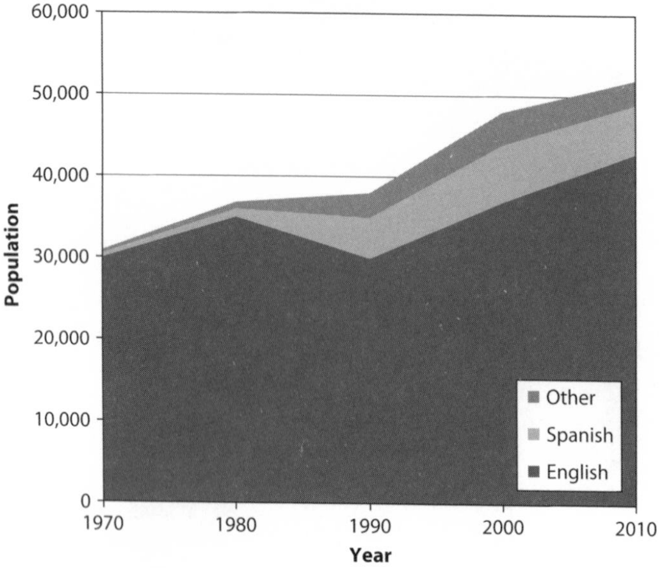

also gives the end user a chance to zoom and filter to areas of highest interest for a more detailed view.

Interactive data visualization can be defined as any visualization that "can be manipulated directly and simply by the user in a free-flowing manner, including such actions as filtering the data and drilling down into details" (Few, 2005, p. 8). Although analysts have long had the ability to filter and manipulate data, only recently has that capability been offered to the wider public and potential evaluation stakeholders. Web applications such as Tableau offer end users the chance to go beyond predefined charts and actively explore data sets. The recent surge in audience-side interactivity follows Schneiderman's (1996) visual information seeking mantra: "Overview first, zoom and filter, then details-on-demand" (p. 2).

The following two examples show what is possible with the help of a good Web developer. Although the sophistication of these visuals may be outside the budget for some evaluators, advancements are bringing technologies closer all the time. Additionally, as large state, federal, and international agencies continue to incorporate visualization into their data releases, evaluators should see an increase in data that are made available in an interactive visual format, ready for analysis.

Oakland Crimespotting. When evaluators develop reports, data visualization often answers key evaluation questions. Although answering those key questions is important and necessary, the underlying data can also answer other specific questions posed by individual stakeholders. Releasing full data

Figure 2.8. Oakland Crimespotting Home Page

sets may open the door, but many individual stakeholders may not have the analytical ability to sort through massive data sets to find their answers.

To open up crime statistics to the broader Oakland community, Stamen Design (2012) developed Oakland Crimespotting, calling it an "interactive map of crimes in Oakland, CA and a tool for understanding crime in cities" (http://www.stamen.com/projects/crimespotting). At the time of this writing there were 100,000 individual crime reports mapped as part of this application, dating back to January 2008. Oakland Crimespotting offers an example of how larger data sets can be released and remain accessible to broader groups of interested stakeholders. With the use of an intuitive interface that allows exploration, residents can find answers to questions such as: What is the frequency of crime reports in a specific neighborhood? Do specific areas see higher crime rates during evening hours?

Reported crimes are mapped and labeled by crime type (based on Oakland's crime statistics categorization). Labels are also color coded, with red corresponding to violent crimes, green to property crimes, and blue to quality of life crimes (see colors in online companion to this volume at www.ndedataviz.com). The map can pan and zoom to show individual locations. Data can be filtered by date, time of day, and crime type (see Figure 2.8).

The Education Nation Scorecard. Quantitative data are best understood when they are placed within context, but the context for a school superintendent is very different from the context for a parent. This poses a challenge for evaluators who have a responsibility to present data to a wide audience. A 95% pass rate for 4th-grade reading tests sounds good, but how does it compare to overall rates in the county and state? How does one

Figure 2.9. Education Nation Scorecard—School View

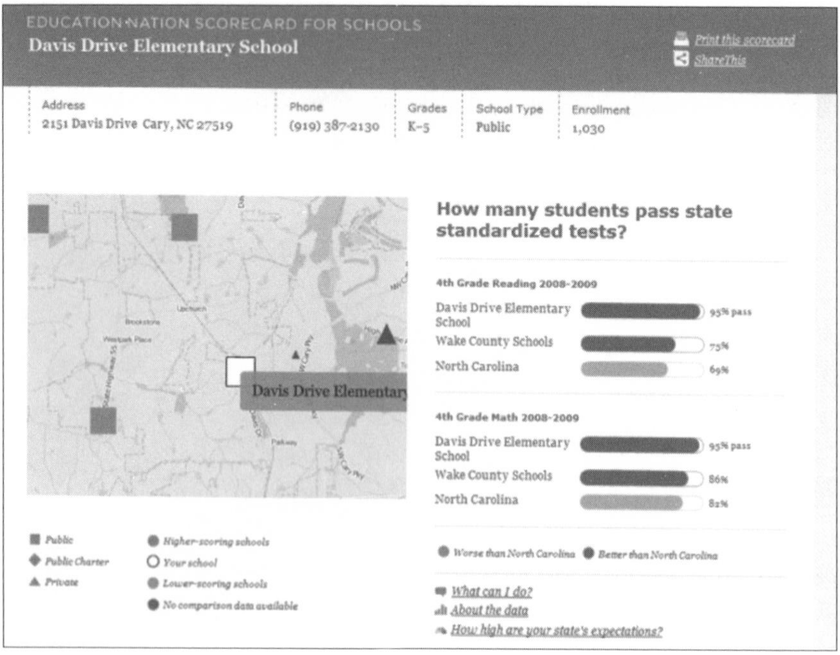

child's school compare to those in surrounding neighborhoods? How is the entire district doing in comparison to other districts?

Interactive data visualization offers evaluators the ability to present data in an appropriate context for many specific audiences. This ability is demonstrated by the Education Nation Scorecard developed by Fathom Information Design. According to the website, "The Education Nation Scorecard allows families to navigate the education system by providing useful, easily understandable information about performance at individual schools, as well as in districts, states, and the nation as a whole" (Fathom Design, 2012).

The interactive website prompts the user to start by finding a specific school. Surrounding schools with higher pass rates on standardized tests are colored blue; schools with lower pass rates on standardized tests are colored orange (Figure 2.9; to view this figure in color please visit www .ndedataviz.com). Shape is used to designate public, public charter, or private schools. Size is used to signify enrollment. Further comparison information is provided, showing the individual school against results for the county and state, such as in Figure 2.10.

Through the creation of interactive visualizations, evaluators will be able to open up large data sets to a much wider audience than would be possible without interactivity. Specific questions posed by stakeholders about topics as diverse as individual schools and city blocks could be answered without an analyst's assistance.

Figure 2.10. Education Nation Scorecard—District View

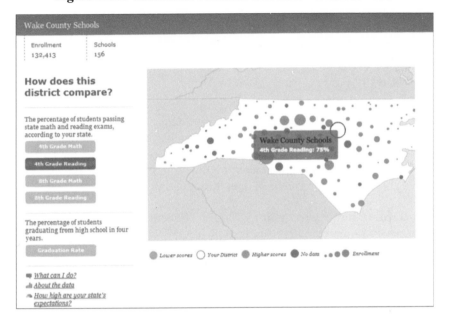

Although the previous examples of interactive display highlight customized visualizations, often built by someone with programming knowledge, there are several applications evaluators without those skills can use to create interactive data visualizations. Tableau Public, IBM's ManyEyes, GeoCommons, and Google Fusion Tables all allow for the creation of charts and maps that let the reader select, zoom, and filter. These applications were designed for presenting data on the Web.

Interactive visualization concerns. The use of interactive visualization is not without its concerns. Interactivity gives the designer less control over the story being told. But there are methods the designer can use to guide the reader down a specific path subtly. Attracting a reader's attention to a specific story within a graphic can be accomplished with the help of visual cues. For example, if an evaluator would like to highlight program sites not meeting performance measure standards, she could set the graphic to display the specific sites in a different color. The default starting point is under the designer's control.

A second concern is about protecting confidentiality. When data are presented in a static table it is easy to identify potentially compromising data, such as small cell sizes that could be used to signal individual respondents. Interactive visualizations can intentionally or unintentionally bury data, which makes it harder to identify potential issues visually. One possible safeguard involves reformatting the original data set prior to connecting it to any visual, where potentially compromising data should be combined to create a full data set that is acceptable for publication. If the underlying data set is shareable the evaluator no longer has to be concerned about the visualization unveiling personally identifiable data.

Animation

As mentioned, one concern regarding interactive visualization is that the evaluator gives up some control over the data presentation to readers, allowing them to create their own story. Although this is helpful in allowing readers to place data within their own personal context, readers can also miss good stories. Through the use of animation, experienced analysts can act as guides, turning visualized data into illustrations for storytelling.

Gapminder. Hans Rosling's (2007) TED conference talk is a prime example of animated data visualization (http://www.gapminder.org/videos/hans-rosling-ted-talk-2007-seemingly-impossible-is-possible/). In the talk, Rosling presented a series of bubble charts spanning decades. The charts were set in motion while Rosling narrated the story illustrated by the data visualization. The result is essentially a guided tour of what was initially an interactive data set (Figure 2.11).

Figure 2.11. Gapminder World

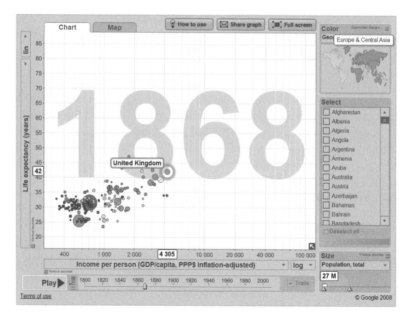

Evaluators with data stories to tell can create their own motion graphics with the use of Gapminder World. At www.gapminder.org visitors can experiment with the same technology used by Hans Rosling. Another option is to use simple and free video editing software, like Windows Movie Maker, to replicate the animation effect. Export a series of visuals in an image format, then string them together with the software. Add voice-over narration and the video will be ready to be uploaded to a Web video hosting site like YouTube.

Animation concerns. One concern with animation is that by setting the chart in motion, the evaluator offers less opportunity for a viewer to soak in any individual graphic. Care must also be taken to see that the story is one that appears through sequence. Tools like Google's Public Data Explorer, which will be discussed below, allow for the data to be paused for exploration at specific points in time.

Automation

Automation refers to the use of programming code to collect, publish, or update data with limited or no human intervention. Thanks to worldwide open data initiatives there has been tremendous growth in the availability of Application Programming Interfaces (APIs), which allow for the direct connection of multiple data sources with the software necessary for visualizing that information. Just a few of the sources with available APIs include social media applications (Twitter), world organizations (World Bank), countries (United Kingdom), states (Oregon), and cities (Chicago). According to Programmable Web (2012), an API cataloguing site, there are close to 5,000 APIs available to those with the expertise required to use them. The massive amount of available data has fueled software developers and led to the creation of visualization applications equipped with pre-established connections to underlying data sources.

In layman's terms, APIs are the mechanisms that allow computers to speak with one another and share information. For the purpose of this chapter, the existence of APIs allows for data to be shared between entities that hold data and entities that visualize that data. Many data sources rely on human intervention for download; APIs are not a given. But when data sources are opened up to developers in a way that allows for connections between software and underlying data sources, new possibilities exist. The ample number of social media visualizations is a by-product both of interesting subject matter and the availability of APIs by sites like Facebook and Twitter.

Twitter API. Most evaluators will experience APIs indirectly through the use of third-party software applications. For example, the Twitter API is utilized by a wide variety of applications. A post on www.aea365.org by Smith (2012) discusses the use of NodeXL, a social network map creator. The post included a map showing connections between Twitter users who

Figure 2.12. NodeXL Social Network Map—#eval Hashtag

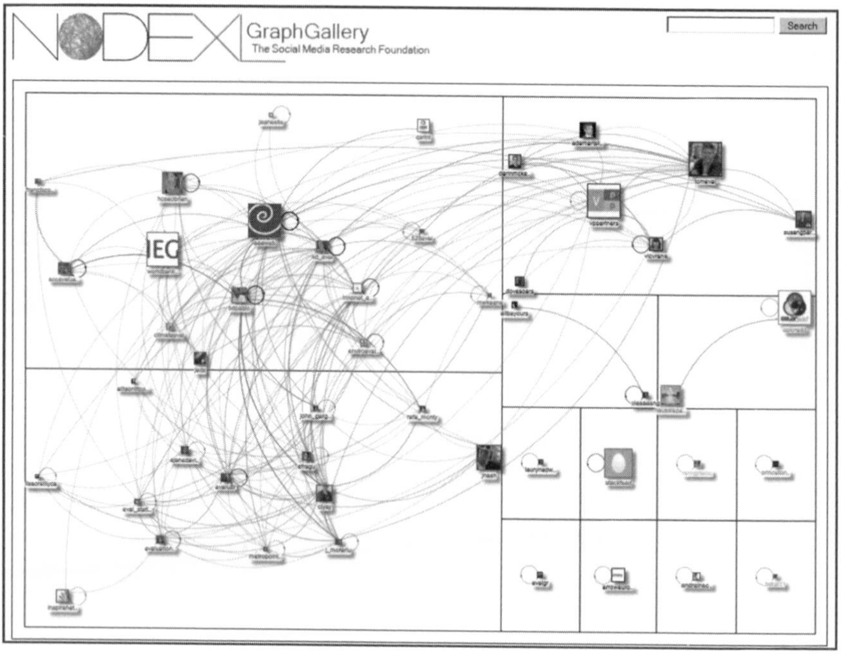

included the hashtag #eval in their tweets. The map was made possible because of a connection to Twitter's streaming API (Figure 2.12).

World Bank API. The World Bank has made much of their data available to software developers through an open API. This creates a pathway for third-party applications to offer alternative visualization tools to those developed directly by the World Bank.

The Indicator API provides access to the following databases: World Development Indicators, Global Development Finance, African Development Indicators, Doing Business, Enterprise Surveys, Millennium Development Goals, Education Statistics, Gender Statistics, Health and Nutrition Statistics, and IDA Results Measurement System. Additionally, there are separate APIs available to gain access to Climate Data and World Bank Finances data.

One of the applications making use of World Bank Data is Google's Public Data Explorer. The tool is available to anyone at http://www.google.com/publicdata and requires no software development. This same tool can also be used to explore data from the U.S. Census Bureau, U.S. Bureau of Labor Statistics, The Centers for Disease Control and Prevention, and many

Figure 2.13. Google's Public Data Explorer

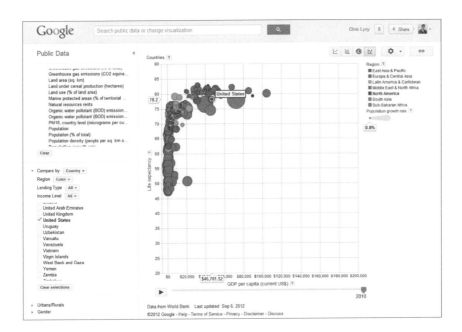

others. Although there is a slight learning curve when one begins to use the tool, you only have to learn once to open yourself up to a wide range of sources (Figure 2.13).

APIs are merely tools that allow for data connections to be made. The vast majority of the time they will go unnoticed by the user. Most evaluators will likely not need to know the technology that goes on behind the scenes of an online data collection, but, as I will mention when discussing concerns below, there are times when understanding the technology is important.

Embedding visualizations. When available, one way to make sure Web-published data visualizations stay current is to use a Web application's embed feature, such as those offered through Tableau Public and ManyEyes. Unlike downloading an image and reposting each time an update is made, embedding a graphic will maintain a live connection to the original source data set. When the source data need to be updated, the embedded graphic will automatically update. This is particularly useful if the same graphic is going to appear in multiple locations across the Web.

Automation concerns. One concern when working with third-party applications is that software-development decisions could impact the validity of the presented data. Just as with other data analyses, the quality of the measurement affects the quality of the analysis. For example, at the time of this writing Twitter offered two separate APIs. Twitter's REST API, which requires less maintenance for the developer, is the more likely of the two to miss tweets. Twitter's streaming API creates a stable connection and has a higher possibility that all, or close to all, tweets will be captured. This is technical, but the important takeaway is that decisions made during the development of an application can have an impact on the validity of presented data. When the analyses are critical, it is important to understand not only if a data set is connected to an underlying source, but how that source was defined and measured.

A second concern is that APIs can allow for the release of large streams of personally identifiable data, sometimes with only tenuous consent. The availability of such data should not dictate the ethics of using the data. There are discussions across the globe over what data should be public and what data should be private. Evaluators should take part in this discussion.

Final Thoughts

The last 15 years have given evaluators some new variations of old chart standards and the software necessary to start using new chart types. All of the examples in part one were created with the use of technology that is either freely available to, or widely used by, evaluators. More importantly though, because of the Web, evaluators are no longer limited to presenting only the material that can fit on a static page. It is now possible to deliver large complex data sets in a format approachable for a wide array of stakeholders. The ability to connect and keep up-to-date through automation can also change the way programs share and access data. But in order to take full advantage of these developments, evaluators need to build their own technical capacity. The technology exists and it is time to start making full use of it to enhance our evaluation practice.

References

Bonnet, D. (1997). Packing it in with horizontal bars. *New Directions for Evaluation, 73*, 9–15.

DeVeaux, M. (1997). Evaluation concerns and the presentation of data. *New Directions for Evaluation, 73*, 69–74.

Fathom Design. (2012). *Education nation scorecard for schools.* Retrieved from http://nbcscorecard.greatschools.org/

Few, S. (2005). *Visual and interactive analytics.* Retrieved from http://www.perceptual edge.com/articles/Whitepapers/Visual_Analytics.pdf

Gargani, J. (2012, February 13). *Should the pie chart be retired?* [Blog]. Retrieved from http://evalblog.com/2012/02/13/should-the-pie-chart-be-retired/

Gemignani, Z. (2006, September 8). *Microcharts, a different take on Excel charting* [Blog]. Retrieved from http://www.juiceanalytics.com/writing/microcharts-a-different-take-on-excel-charting/

Henry, G. T., & Dolan, K. (1997). Conclusion: Keys to good graphing. *New Directions for Evaluation, 73*, 101–105.

Kerin, A. (2010). *Twitter sparkline generator!* Retrieved from http://www.datadriven consulting.com/2010/06/twitter-sparkline-generator/

ProgrammableWeb. (2012). Retrieved from http://www.programmableweb.com/

Rosling, H. (2007). *The seemingly impossible is possible* [Video file]. Retrieved from http://www.gapminder.org/videos/hans-rosling-ted-talk-2007-seemingly-impossible-is-possible

Schneiderman, B. (1996). *The eyes have it: A task by data type taxonomy for information visualizations.* College Park, MD: Institute for Systems Research. Retrieved from http://drum.lib.umd.edu/bitstream/1903/5784/1/TR_96–66.pdf

Smith, M. (2012, March 30). *Marc Smith on using NodeXL* [Blog]. Retrieved from http://aea365.org/blog/?p=5953

Stamen Design (2012). *Oakland crimespotting.* Retrieved from http://oakland.crime spotting.org/

Tufte, E. R. (2006). *Beautiful evidence.* Cheshire, CT: Graphics Press.

CHRISTOPHER LYSY is a research analyst at Westat, where he is involved with several federal special education evaluations.

Henderson, S., & Segal, E. H. (2013). Visualizing qualitative data in evaluation research. In T. Azzam & S. Evergreen (Eds.), *Data visualization, part 1. New Directions for Evaluation, 139*, 53–71.

3

Visualizing Qualitative Data in Evaluation Research

Stuart Henderson, Eden H. Segal

Abstract

This chapter introduces data visualization techniques for qualitative data. These techniques can be used in most stages of evaluations, including early planning and design, data analysis, and reporting. Qualitative data visualization can also be used in different approaches to evaluation, for instance, traditional process and summative, developmental, utilization, participatory, and mixed-methods evaluations. The authors first describe a conceptual framework for understanding the different types of qualitative data visualizations before providing examples of visualizations in various evaluation

We thank the editors of this issue, Tarek Azzam and Stephanie Evergreen, for their generous feedback and suggestions. We also appreciate the valuable feedback from Daniel Dohan, Julie Rainwater, Cynthia Robins, David Segal, and Mady Wechsler Segal. Parts of this project were supported by the National Center for Advancing Translational Sciences (NCATS), National Institutes of Health (NIH), through Grant UL1 TR000002.

Note: The figures presented in this chapter can be viewed in color by accessing www.NDEdataviz.com and selecting Chapter 3.

contexts. The chapter concludes with a discussion of challenges or issues evaluators should consider when visualizing qualitative data. © Wiley Periodicals, Inc., and the American Evaluation Association.

Much data visualization guidance centers on how to represent and analyze quantitative data visually. One may look, for example, to the work of Tufte (1983, 1990, 2006) and Few (2004, 2009), whose writings have been frequently cited by the other authors in this volume and throughout the field. Less attention has been paid to how to display qualitative or text data visually (for exceptions see Miles & Huberman, 1994; Clarke, 2005; and Wheeldon & Ahlberg, 2012). This may be in part because qualitative work focuses on explaining the "why" and "how" of complex phenomena, which are not easily portrayed with images. Guidance on ways to use visualization techniques is especially limited for evaluators who use qualitative research methods. This chapter introduces different approaches to visualization and offers suggestions for evaluators on how and when to represent qualitative data visually.

In this chapter we review established techniques for visualizing qualitative data (such as matrices and mapping) and explore a variety of newer ways that evaluators can portray their qualitative data, such as word clouds, tree representations, and spectrum displays. Throughout, we point out strengths and weaknesses of the different approaches for evaluation purposes.

We start with an overview of qualitative data and how it traditionally has been displayed. Second, we introduce a framework for organizing and understanding visualizations of qualitative data. Third, we present examples of qualitative data visualization, specifically using evaluation data. And finally, we discuss challenges and unavoidable trade-offs when translating text data into visuals.

As important as identifying what this chapter covers it is worth noting what it does not cover. Because we are focused specifically on creating and using visual representations of text data, we do not discuss the field of visual methods (the collection or use of visual images, such as photographs or art). The chapter is also not meant to provide an exhaustive inventory of visualizations of qualitative data. Instead, we focus on visualizations that evaluators might use in their daily practice and that they can create on their own using minimal specialized software. Of course, we hope that by highlighting both the logic and possibilities for visualizing qualitative data, evaluators can build on the ideas we set forth, expand the ways qualitative data are visualized, and ultimately increase the range and utility of available approaches.

Evaluation Use of Qualitative Visualizations

The visualization techniques discussed here can be used in most stages of evaluations, including early planning with stakeholders, data analysis, and reporting. However, throughout the chapter we highlight that some visualizations lend themselves better to early phases of the evaluation (e.g., word clouds and word trees) and others to later phases (e.g., maps and matrices). The visualization of qualitative data can also be used with different approaches to evaluation, such as formative and summative, developmental, utilization, participatory, and mixed-methods evaluations. In fact, any evaluation that includes a qualitative component may benefit from the additional perspectives and insights that a visual representation of the data can provide.

Traditional Display of Qualitative Data

Evaluators routinely collect a variety of qualitative data as part of their evaluation research, including open-ended survey responses, interview and focus group transcripts, observational notes, secondary data from organizations (e.g., reports, strategic plans, and policy documents), photographs, videos, and more recently social media communication, such as Twitter feeds and e-mail correspondence (Patton, 2002). A common way of presenting qualitative information is to select multiple, illustrative excerpts of the data to highlight dominant themes or ideas. For instance, in a case study of a program seeking to improve prospective teachers' interest in and readiness to teach science and mathematics in high-need urban classrooms, new interns discuss their perceptions about urban schools. One frequent theme that arose during in-depth interviews was that interns' perceptions were influenced by media portrayals of urban youth. For example, a White middle-class intern, who was assisting in an 8th-grade all-Black charter classroom, said:

> I've never been in an inner-city school in Baltimore so maybe I'm just being biased, maybe I've seen *The Wire* too many times. … Teachers set a very low bar and they pass them, which I've heard happens in a lot of public schools.

Quotes in participants' own words, such as the above, can illustrate the nuance, complexity, and depth of individuals' beliefs and actions. Importantly, they also provide an opportunity to honor and highlight participants' voices, an important goal in many evaluation approaches.

Capturing the essence and meaning of text data is a major strength of interview and report excerpts (Grbich, 2007); however, they can be less effective at communicating broader views of data and may be seen as lacking the analytic power or credibility of quantitative data displays (Slone, 2009). In addition, multiple or long excerpts can be a "cumbersome form of display" (Miles & Huberman, 1994, p. 91). An alternative way to present text is through visual displays. Visual representations of qualitative data can reduce and focus text, providing a structure to identify patterns and outliers, or introduce new levels of understanding (Miles & Huberman, 1994;

Onwuegbuzie & Dickinson, 2008). The challenge is adding structure to the data without oversimplifying or misrepresenting them and without losing the subtle meanings or emotions rooted in them. As we will show, one way to manage these challenges is to develop visualizations that include or integrate visuals and text (Miles & Huberman, 1994).

Framework for Visualizing Qualitative Data

To explore the range of data visualization for text, we construct a framework for understanding and organizing different options (Figure 3.1). In most visual representations of qualitative data, the data are broken down into segments such as individual words, sentences, themes, or less often, whole narratives (Bernard & Ryan, 2010). These segments, or what we will refer to as the "level of display," allow for the possibility of counting, cataloguing, or

Figure 3.1. Graph Showing Variety of Qualitative Visualizations by Display and Complexity

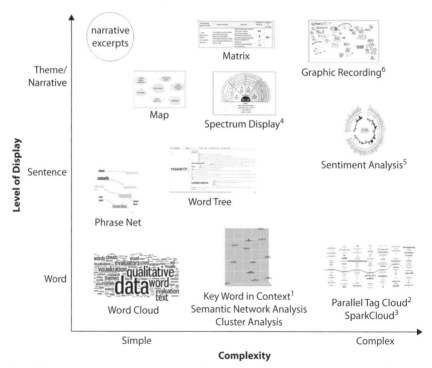

Notes: [1]For more information see Bernard and Ryan (2010), image created with NVivo; [2]Collins, Viégas, and Wattenberg (2009); [3]Lee, Riche, Karlson, and Carpendale (2010); [4]Slone (2009); [5]Smith (2011), www.openbible.info; [6]Dean-Coffey (in press).

connecting with other segments. Importantly, how the text is segmented impacts the visuals an evaluator can create. For example, when evaluators are interested in visually representing the story of program participants' experiences, they must make a decision whether to highlight individual words, sentences, or general themes. The level of display is represented on the vertical axis of the framework. On the horizontal axis, we have rated the complexity of the visualization from simple to complex. The degree of complexity does not refer to the complexity of what is seen in the visualization, but rather the knowledge or skill level required to develop the visualization. Thus, available platforms to create word clouds, shown in the bottom left portion of Figure 3.1, can make images that appear complex, yet are simple to create and require little analysis to understand. Conversely, visualizations in the top right portion of Figure 3.1, such as complex matrices, are more difficult to create and also require more sophisticated data analysis.

In the examples that follow, we use data from evaluation research to illustrate data visualizations at each of level of display and highlight how they can be used throughout the evaluation process.

Examples of Visualizations of Qualitative Data

Word

At the most basic level, text data can be segmented into individual words. Researchers in the humanities and other fields might use this approach to explore word use in novels, political speeches, and historical records. For example, an exploration of words used in all of Shakespeare's works, maintained by opensourceShakespeare, indicates that the word *death* shows up in 844 entries, whereas *birth* appears in 103 instances (www.opensourceshakespeare.org). To go further with text analysis, multidimensional scaling and cluster analysis (Bernard & Ryan, 2010) could be used to find patterns in text.[1] Although there is and has been software to identify and analyze words in text, it has been only recently that word counts have become easy to display visually in word or tag clouds through popular online applications, such as Wordle (www.wordle.net) or TagCrowd (www.tagcrowd.com).

Word clouds provide a visual display of word counts from one or more texts. The more frequently a word appears, the larger the word is displayed in a word cloud visual (Viégas & Wattenberg, 2008). So, for example, in Figure 3.2, which is a word cloud of this article, the words *data, qualitative,* and *visualization* were frequently used words.[2] Color, font type, and the shape of word clouds can be changed for different effects.

Word clouds create a dramatic visual, which likely accounts for their popularity. In fact, when evaluators hear of the idea of visualizing qualitative data, a word cloud may be the first thing that comes to mind. However,

Figure 3.2. Word Cloud Displaying the Most Frequently Used Words in This Article

Source: Created with Wordle (www.wordle.net).

significant concerns have been brought up about their use. The main issue raised regarding word clouds is that they rely purely on the frequency of word usage. They do not provide context for audiences to understand how the word was used within the text (Harris, 2011). For example, a word cloud is unable to differentiate between words with positive or negative connotations, and it does not provide information about the surrounding words, which may influence understanding. A second concern is that word clouds can be visually misleading. Longer words take more space within the visualization, resulting in "undue emphasis over shorter ones" (Viégas & Wattenberg, 2008, p. 51).

Despite concerns with word clouds, their ease of creation and striking visuals make them a useful tool for evaluators if they are used sparingly and their challenges are acknowledged. They can be used in early stages of evaluation planning and design to show stakeholders frequently used words found in strategic planning or development documents. Although less useful for complex analysis, they can be used in the early stages of analysis to help evaluators identify descriptive key words in interview and focus group transcripts or to compare multiple data sets or transcripts (Weisgerber & Butler, 2009). For example, two or more word clouds can be shown together to contrast word usage in the documents. Advanced visualizations, such as parallel tag clouds (Collins et al., 2009) and sparkclouds (Lee, Riche, Karlson, & Carpendale, 2010), are recent developments that allow users to compare multiple word clouds. Finally, when coupled with explanations, word clouds might be used in the reporting stage of evaluation to illustrate domi-nant ideas or themes for lay audiences.

One significant improvement to make word clouds stronger for evalu-ation and dampen some of the legitimate concerns raised about their use would be to link the individual words to the underlying text (either manu-ally or digitally). This would provide the missing context to which critics of word clouds have called attention. Such linkages also would bring this type of visualization more closely in line with the traditions, values, and priorities of many evaluators using qualitative approaches, including the important emphasis on the unique perspectives and language that partici-pants choose. Examples of this are the *New York Times* interactive word count visualizations of the 2012 Republican and Democratic conventions. These word clouds link each word depicted in the visual back to the text containing the word (Bostock, Carter, & Ericson, 2012; Bostock & Ericson, 2012). This capability has been added to many of the computer-assisted qualitative data analysis software (CAQDAS) programs, such as NVivo, ATLAS.ti, Dedoose, and MAXQDA, although the end user may need the software program to use the interactive features.

Sentences

Moving beyond the word level, text can be displayed in sentences or short phrases. The two main visual tools at this level are word trees and phrase nets. These tools, originally developed by IBM's project Many Eyes (www -958.ibm.com), *but now available in some qualitative software programs,* allow users to see how a particular word is used in sentences or phrases. Word tree programs provide a visual display of the connection of an identified word(s) to other words in text data through a branching system (Wattenberg & Viégas, 2008). Users can have the tree branch to words that come before or after the identified word. This visualization provides some context for words, which is an improvement over word clouds, and also provides a sense of how frequently certain words are used. For example, in a study that examined the relationship between a research university and commu-nity organizations, we found that the understandings and goals of research varied. In a word tree created from the study's documents (Figure 3.3), we can view all the sentences that contain the word *research* to provide a better understanding of how this word was used and the variation of its use.

Phrase nets differ from word trees in that they highlight the connec-tions of word pairs rather than whole sentences (van Ham, Wattenberg, & Viégas, 2009). For instance, in Figure 3.4, which uses the same text as Figure 3.3, the words that are paired with *research* in the documents are displayed, with the size of the word indicating frequency like in a word cloud. The arrows show that both *collaboration* and *distrust* were used by respondents when discussing research and researchers, visually highlight-ing the multiple interpretations and meanings of research.

NEW DIRECTIONS FOR EVALUATION • DOI: 10.1002/ev

Figure 3.3. Word Tree of an Evaluation Document Exploring the Role of Research in Community Organizations

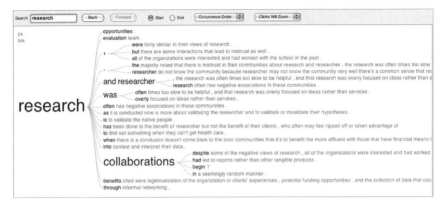

Source: Created with Many Eyes (www-958.ibm.com).

Figure 3.4. Phrase Net of an Evaluation Document Exploring the Role of Research in Community Organizations

Source: Created with Many Eyes (www-958.ibm.com).

NEW DIRECTIONS FOR EVALUATION • DOI: 10.1002/ev

Although sentence visualization tools provide more contextual information than single word analysis, the information is still limited. For evaluation purposes, visual representations of sentences have similar uses as word clouds and, if their limitations are recognized, they can be useful supports for evaluation design, analysis, and reporting. Their strongest use is for exploratory data analysis (Weisgerber & Butler, 2009). By exploring key words within sentences, evaluators can identify if there are consistent patterns of word use or whether words are being used in divergent ways within a text or multiple texts.

Themes

A common approach for making qualitative data understandable is identifying themes within a text (Ryan & Bernard, 2003). Evaluators and researchers can group and connect the identified themes to present broader ideas and theories about the general pattern of stories within the data. Since the process of identifying themes requires evaluators to conduct analysis, the visualization of themes is most valuable in the analysis and reporting stage of an evaluation and less useful for planning or data collection.

Visualizing data at the theme level offers more options and dimensions for visual representations than at the word or sentence/phrase level. Visualizations of words or sentences are limited to frequency of a single word or correlation between words, but at the thematic level, evaluators can also examine attributes, such as intensity or type. For instance, evaluators can rank themes as low/high or place themes into nonordinal categories. Furthermore, with themes, the dimensions of frequency, correlations, or quality can be used separately or they can be integrated into a single visualization.

To demonstrate these ideas more concretely, the following three examples use a single set of data to illustrate a variety of ways themes can be visually represented. The data presented come from hypothetical semistructured interviews of research trainees who had achieved career success after participating in an academic training program. The matrix in Figure 3.5 lists themes, derived from interviews and the literature, associated with trainee success. For instance, the first row shows the theme *mentor support*, whereas the second row is the theme *pilot funding*. Each column represents one trainee: Iv1 is a successful trainee, Iv2 is a second trainee, and so on. Each box in the matrix represents the presence of the theme, with darker shading indicating a higher importance. The shading could be determined through intensity (e.g., by having multiple coders rate the degree to which the theme was present) or through frequency (e.g., how often the theme was mentioned in each interview). This type of matrix allows evaluators to assess visually which themes were most prominent (in this case, mentor support, pilot funding, and grant writing support) as well as the major factors that led to success for each individual trainee. For instance, Trainee 3 did not find participation in the training program helpful, although *early*

Figure 3.5. Matrix Displaying the Level of Importance of Themes Uncovered in Interviews With Training Program Participants

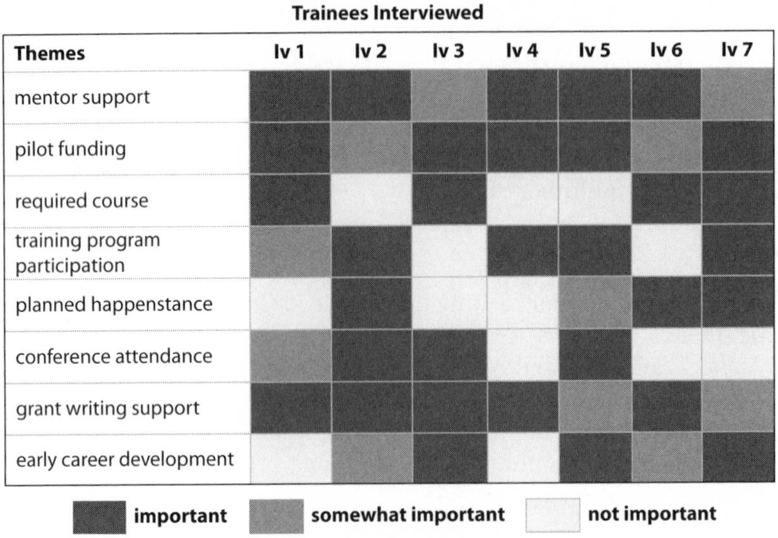

Trainees Interviewed

Themes	Iv 1	Iv 2	Iv 3	Iv 4	Iv 5	Iv 6	Iv 7
mentor support							
pilot funding							
required course							
training program participation							
planned happenstance							
conference attendance							
grant writing support							
early career development							

■ important   ■ somewhat important   □ not important

Note: Iv# is the number of each trainee. Darker shades indicate increased importance of theme.

career development was important to her success. Similar to a cluster heat map (Wilkinson & Friendly, 2009) or an ethnoarray (Dohan, Abramson, & Miller, 2012), a benefit of this visual is that it provides an overview of the patterns within individual cases and allows for easy comparison between cases. This information can be used for presenting or reporting to external audiences and also for internal program improvement.

One concern that many qualitative researchers might have with the visualization in Figure 3.5 is that the qualitative data has been quantified. In other words, the matrix does not provide the stories or context behind the themes. This is a valid critique. Ideally, when creating matrices or other visualizations, evaluators should link the individual boxes to quotes that support viewer understanding of the theme. For instance, associated with the early career development for Trainee 3 (Iv3), there could be one or more illustrative quotes such as, "I was fortunate to receive pilot funding, excellent grant-writing support, and some opportunities to present research and obtain directed feedback from mentors and peers at a critically important time, early in my career development." As with CAQDAS packages' increased capabilities with word clouds, most qualitative software packages have the ability to create a matrix based on theme frequency with links to the corresponding text within the program.

Figures 3.6 and 3.7 show two additional ways—mapping and chronological charting—to represent the academic training program data. In Figure 3.6, the focus is on the connection and relationship between themes rather

Figure 3.6. Map Highlighting the Connection of Themes for Individuals Who Were Successful in an Academic Training Program

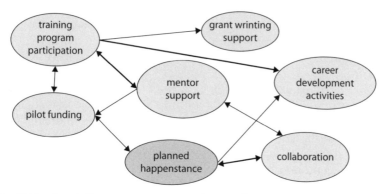

Note: Thicker lines indicate a greater connection between themes.

Figure 3.7. Chronological Charts From Interviews With Individuals Who Were Successful in an Academic Training Program

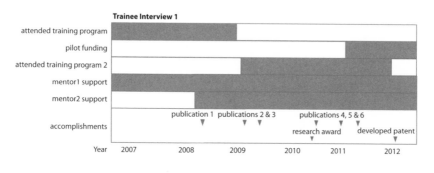

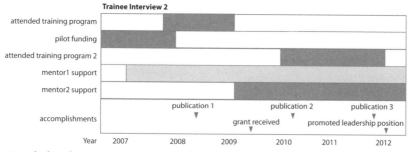

Note: Shading denotes presence of activity. Lighter shading represents lower intensity of activity.

NEW DIRECTIONS FOR EVALUATION • DOI: 10.1002/ev

than individual trainees, as was depicted in Figure 3.5. This thematic map is similar to a mind map or concept map, familiar to many evaluators (Trochim, 1989; Wheeldon & Ahlberg, 2012). The arrows indicate the direction of influence and can be made different thicknesses to signify the degree of connection if that information is available. Maps can be easily created for data analysis and reporting with standard or specialized software. In addition, Wheeldon and Faubert (2009) highlight their use in data collection.

Figure 3.7 illustrates a chronological chart (Hiller, 2011), which is particularly useful for data that occur over time. This example visually represents two scientific trainees' activities in the training program and their major accomplishments. The shading on each row highlights when each activity occurred. The top chart shows the accomplishments of Trainee 1, who attended a training program from 2007 to 2009 and a second program from 2009 to 2012. We can compare this to Trainee 2, who attended programs from 2008 to 2009 and 2010 to 2012. If multiple chronological charts are displayed, this visualization can be particularly valuable for identifying patterns and making comparisons between cases and, like the Figure 3.5 matrix, would be useful for exploratory analysis or internal reporting to stakeholders for purposes of program improvement.

Another approach for presenting qualitative data at the theme level is the spectrum display (Slone, 2009). Similar to the matrix in Figure 3.5, the spectrum shows individual cases along with themes or categories. The spectrum display in Figure 3.8 shows summarized data collected from open-ended interviews and observations of how 34 library computer users spent their time (Slone, 2009). The outer labels, P1 to P34, are the individual cases, where P1 is person 1 and P34 is person 34. There is a row for each activity, such as e-mail or job search. If a person participated in the activity the box contains a dark circle. The spectrum, unlike the matrix, includes a mutually exclusive variable, in this case "duration," which allows the cases to be ordered. The ordering of cases provides an additional level of analysis. For instance, at a glance we can see that about half of the library patrons who used the computers for 25 minutes or less were signing up or paying bills. However, only 1 patron who used the library computer for more than 25 minutes completed these activities. In addition, the most common goal for individuals who used the computer for over 30 minutes was job-related activity.

To demonstrate various ways of visualizing themes in qualitative evaluation further, we share a thematic conceptual matrix (Miles & Huberman, 1994) and map from the second author's case study of an urban field experience for prospective teachers, which was described briefly in a previous section. With the use of the framework depicted in Figure 3.1, these examples would fall in the upper right portion of the graph, at the theme display level and near the end of the complexity scale. Although they are straightforward to create, the matrix and map communicate several ideas within

Figure 3.8. Spectrum Display of Library Users' Goals in Relation to Search Duration

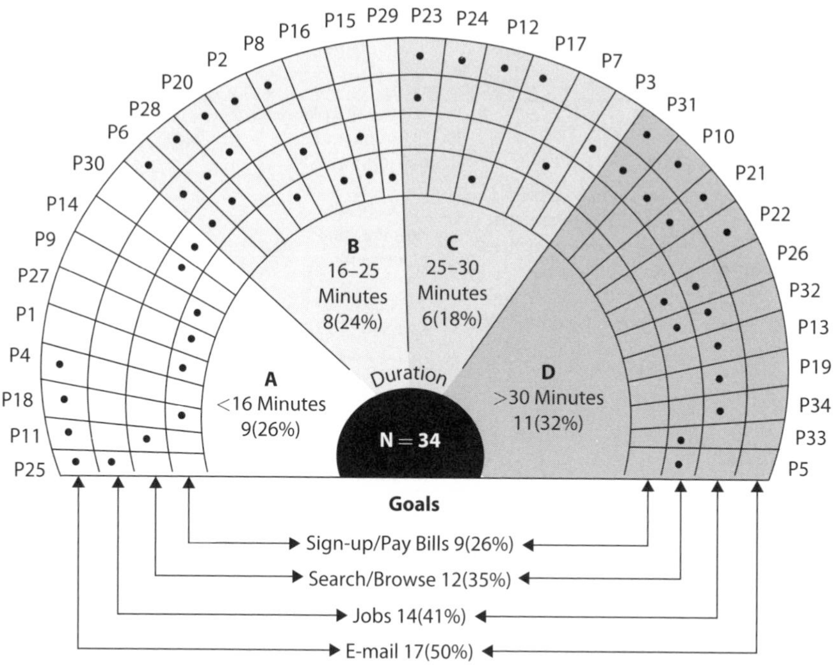

Note: P(#) is the number assigned to each participant.

Source: From Slone (2009). Reprinted with permission.

the visualization, requiring significant analytic and moderate visualizing skills.

Figure 3.9 shows a thematic conceptual matrix of one theoretically based principle, "field experiences explore sociocultural diversity," that was identified through a literature review (Segal, 2011). The figure consists of the principle, the description of the principle, and the four major elements that make up the principle. It also contains symbols that visually indicate the amount of evidence for each element. The visualization's strength is that it highlights the complexity of the findings. By showing that the main principle was present, but some of its elements had countervailing evidence, it maintains the contradictions found in the data in a succinct way. The complete set of visuals showing the study's findings on the nine principles was two pages. In comparison, the traditional textual discussion of the relevant data and conclusions required 13 pages.

As has been discussed in examples throughout this chapter, the symbols in Figure 3.9 could be integrated with supporting text. For instance, in

Figure 3.9. Matrix of the Principle of Sociocultural Diversity and Its Four Elements in a Study of Urban Classrooms

Theoreticall y-based Principle	Excerpt of Principle	Elements	Evidence of Elements	Evidence of Principles
1. Field Experiences Explore Sociocultural Diversity	The program provides carefully planned and varied field experiences that explore sociocultural diversity in schools and communities (Zeichner et al., 1998, p. 168).	1.1. Careful placement planning and monitoring	⊙ ⊘	
		1.2. Careful preparation for placement	⊙	
		1.3. Placement site focused on culturally responsive teaching	●	● ⊘
		1.4. Reflection guided by culturally competent, relevant, responsive educators	● ⊘	

● Evident (at least one notable event/comment, all/most observations/interviews, all participants; OR more than one notable event/comment, most observations/interviews, most participants)

⊙ Partially evident (at least one notable event/comment, all or most participants)

⊘ Not evident/countervailing evidence (more than one notable event/comment that element is not present) (can coexist with other signals)

Note: The symbols indicate the presence of each element.

the example above, the symbol ● in the "evidence of principles" column could be linked to quotes that provide positive evidence:

> I always come to see [Program staff] to check in. I like to come and stop by and say hi because she makes it really easy to just come talk to her. (PCS placement participant)

Similarly, the symbol ⊘ could reveal quotes showing the countervailing evidence as determined by analysis:

> They just asked me would you like a [Program] Fellow, and I said, sure …
> I think it was [school coordinator]. And that was it. (Mentor teacher 1)

With the use of the same evaluation data and findings, Figure 3.10 depicts the text data integrated directly within the visual. The right portion is a graphic of all findings related to the principle, "field experiences explore sociocultural diversity," whereas the left portion includes some of

New Directions for Evaluation • DOI: 10.1002/ev

Figure 3.10. Map of the Principle of Sociocultural Diversity and Its Five Elements in a Study of Urban Classrooms

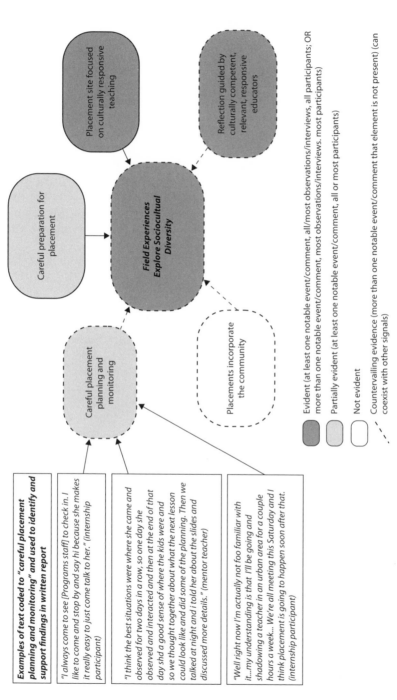

Note: The text in the boxes on the right provides evidence of the element.

the text data that provided evidence for the theme. The darker shading represents a greater level of evidence and the dashed lines around and connecting the shapes show that countervailing evidence was found. Providing illustrative excerpts within the visual, as shown in Figure 3.10, provides the benefit of creating an image that is self-contained. This may be especially relevant and useful for paper-copy evaluation reports. The number of examples and quotes an evaluator can use in this type of visual is limited, however.

The approach shown in Figures 3.9 and 3.10—specifically, the clear connection between the data and the conclusions drawn on multiple dimensions—retains the complexity of qualitative or mixed-methods data. It is useful both for deepening the analysis process and building the capacity of a range of stakeholders to understand and use evaluation findings. Moreover, an approach such as this, one that connects the big picture with the data, can increase the validity of conclusions and provide a way to integrate qualitative and quantitative findings.

Challenges and Conclusions

Visualizing qualitative data presents both logistical and methodological challenges. Logistically, many of the free visualization tools available, such as Many Eyes, do not allow data to remain private and secure—an important criterion for many evaluators and their stakeholders (Weisgerber & Butler, 2009). In addition, the easiest and simplest tools for evaluators to use, for instance, word cloud applications, may not be the most informative for evaluation purposes. Finally, evaluators may not have—or have access to—the computer programming knowledge and skills required to design or produce more advanced and sophisticated interactive visualizations of qualitative data effectively.

Methodologically, the majority of visualization techniques ultimately transform qualitative data into quantifiable segments—an approach that is often the antithesis of the goals of qualitative research methods (Patton, 2002). Done poorly, some visualizations might distract from the meaning and power of text rather than add to reader insight. As previously noted, visual transformation of qualitative data may result in lost emotional tone, meaning, or richness of the data. Thus, evaluators considering visually representing their text data should think carefully about whether it improves the clarity and utility of their analysis and findings. If it does not, then it might be more appropriate to rely on text excerpts or longer narratives to explore and share the material. Evaluators must also be aware of oversimplifying complex text data. The value of qualitative data often lies in its ambiguity and subtleties. Creating a visual representation of text data may lead to the impression that findings are cleaner and less messy than they actually are. Finally, the use of unfamiliar approaches to visualizing qualitative data may require educating audiences on how to interpret them effectively.

NEW DIRECTIONS FOR EVALUATION • DOI: 10.1002/ev

As is true in all reporting, evaluators should consider their audiences and their comfort with data when determining the best way to present.

How much evaluators should integrate visual representation of the qualitative data with text data is an area for discussion. Miles and Huberman (1994) provide reasonable advice, cautioning qualitative researchers to balance their use of narrative and visuals, and although they see specific guidelines as arbitrary, they write, "[W]e would surely be unhappy with 95% story and 5% conceptual, and the converse would be worse" (p. 302). It is likely the same for evaluators who are visualizing qualitative data. A visual without some text data is not going to be as convincing to stakeholders, or as useful for developing analysis, as a visual that includes some narrative data to support it.

Despite these challenges and cautions, finding innovative approaches to represent qualitative texts visually provides opportunities for evaluators to interact with and think about their data differently and to share their results in ways that can introduce new insights. This chapter highlighted the logic one needs to consider when visually representing text with the purpose of stimulating thinking rather than prescribing definitive paths. Many ways exist to represent qualitative data. For instance, we did not include path or network diagrams (Durland & Fredericks, 2005), decision trees (Bernard & Ryan, 2010; Miles & Huberman, 1994), or more advanced visualizations such as sentiment analysis (Gregory et al., 2006). The field of visualization is developing rapidly, and this includes visualizing qualitative data. We encourage evaluators to be open to the many new possibilities that arise and hope that this chapter serves as an introduction that allows them to make sense of the innovations in this area and to think creatively about how they might visually represent their qualitative data.

Notes

1. For examples and discussion of using word counts in data analysis, including key word in context (KWIC) and semantic network analysis, see Bernard and Ryan (2010).
2. Most word cloud software automatically excludes common words, such as *the*. Some also provide the option for users to individualize the exclusion list, group similar words, or create two-word clouds.

References

Bernard, H., & Ryan, G. (2010). *Analyzing qualitative data: Systematic approaches*. Thousand Oaks, CA: Sage.

Bostock, M., Carter, S., & Ericson, M. (2012, September 4). At the Democratic convention, the words being used. *The New York Times*. Retrieved from http://www.nytimes.com/interactive/2012/09/04/us/politics/democratic-convention-words.html?ref=politics

Bostock, M., & Ericson, M. (2012, August 30). At the Republican convention, the words being used. *The New York Times*. Retrieved from http://www.nytimes.com/interactive/2012/08/28/us/politics/convention-word-counts.html#Success

Clarke, A. (2005). *Situational analysis: Grounded theory after the postmodern turn.* Thousand Oaks, CA: Sage.

Collins, C., Viégas, F., & Wattenberg, M. (2009). *Parallel tag clouds to explore and analyze faceted text corpora.* Paper presented at the IEEE Symposium on Visual Analytics Science and Technology, Atlantic City, NJ.

Dean-Coffey, J. (in press). Graphic recording. *New Directions for Evaluation.*

Dohan, D., Abramson, C. M., & Miller, S. (2012, March). *Beyond text: Using arrays of ethnographic data to identify causes and construct narratives.* Unpublished paper presented at the American Journal of Sociology Conference on Causal Thinking and Ethnographic Research, University of Chicago, Chicago, IL. Retrieved from https://sites.google.com/site/ajs2012conference/2011-ieee-ss

Durland, M. M., & Fredericks, K. A. (Eds.). (2005). Social network analysis in program evaluation [Special issue]. *New Directions for Evaluation, 107.*

Few, S. (2004). *Show me the numbers: Designing tables and graphs to enlighten.* Oakland, CA: Analytics Press.

Few, S. (2009). *Now you see it: Simple visualizations techniques for quantitative analysis.* Oakland, CA: Analytics Press.

Grbich, C. (2007). *Qualitative data analysis: An introduction.* Thousand Oaks, CA: Sage.

Gregory, M. L., Chinchor, N., Whitney, P., Carter, R., Hetzler, E., & Turner, A. (2006, July). User-directed sentiment analysis: Visualizing the affective content of documents. In *Proceedings of the Workshop on Sentiment and Subjectivity in Text* (pp. 23–30). Association for Computational Linguistics.

Harris, J. (2011, October 13). Word clouds considered harmful. *Nieman Journalism Lab.* Retrieved from http://www.niemanlab.org/2011/10/word-clouds-considered-harmful/

Hiller, P. (2011). Visualizing the intersection of the personal and the social context: The use of multi-layered chronological charts in biographical studies. *The Qualitative Report, 16*(4), 1018–1033. Retrieved from http://www.nova.edu/ssss/QR/QR16-4/hiller.pdf

Lee, B., Riche, N., Karlson, A. K., & Carpendale, S. (2010). SparkClouds: Visualizing trends in tag clouds. *IEEE Transactions on Visualization and Computer Graphics, 16*(6), 1182–1189.

Miles, M. B., & Huberman, A. M. (1994). *Qualitative data analysis.* Thousand Oaks, CA: Sage.

Onwuegbuzie, A., & Dickinson, W. (2008). Mixed methods analysis and information visualization: Graphical display for effective communication of research results. *The Qualitative Report, 13*(2), 204–225. Retrieved from http://www.nova.edu/ssss/QR/QR13-2/onwuegbuzie.pdf

Patton, M. Q. (2002). *Qualitative research and evaluation method* (3rd ed.). Thousand Oaks, CA: Sage.

Ryan, G. W., & Bernard, H. R. (2003). Techniques to identify themes. *Field Methods, 15*(1), 85–109.

Segal, E. H. (2011). *Early urban field experiences for prospective teachers: A case study of multicultural field placements through a university-based preservice STEM teacher program* (Doctoral dissertation). Available from ProQuest Dissertations and Theses database. (UMI 3495409)

Slone, D. J. (2009). Visualizing qualitative information. *The Qualitative Report, 14*(3), 488–497. Retrieved from http://www.nova.edu/ssss/QR/QR14-3/slone.pdf

Smith, J. (2011). Applying sentiment analysis to the bible. Retrieved from http://www.openbible.info/blog/2011/10/applying-sentiment-analysis-to-the-bible/

Trochim, W. M. (1989). An introduction to concept mapping for planning and evaluation. *Evaluation and Program Planning, 12*(1), 1–16.

Tufte, E. R. (1983). *The visual display of quantitative information.* Chesire, CT: Graphics Press.

Tufte, E. R (1990). *Envisioning information.* Cheshire, CT: Graphics Press.

Tufte, E. R. (2006). *Beautiful evidence.* Cheshire, CT: Graphics Press.

Van Ham, F., Wattenberg, M., & Viégas, F. (2009). Mapping text with phrase nets. *IEEE Transactions on Visualizations and Computer Graphics, 15*(6):1169–1176.

Viégas, F., & Wattenberg, M. (2008). Tag clouds and the case for vernacular visualization. *ACM Interactions, 15*(4), 49–52.

Wattenberg, M., & Viégas, F. (2008). The word tree, an interactive visual concordance. *IEEE Transaction on Visualization and Computer Graphics, 14*(6), 1221–1228.

Weisgerber, C., & Butler, S. (2009). Visualizing the future of interaction studies: Data visualization applications as a research, pedagogical, and presentational tool for interaction scholars. *The Electronic Journal of Communication, 19*(1/2). Retrieved from http://www.cios.org/ejcpublic/019/1/019125.HTML

Wheeldon, J., & Ahlberg, M. (2012). *Visualizing social science research.* Thousand Oaks, CA: Sage.

Wheeldon, J., & Faubert, J. (2009). Framing experience: Concept maps, mind maps, and data collection in qualitative research. *International Journal of Qualitative Methods, 8*(3), 68–83.

Wilkinson, L., & Friendly, M. (2009). The history of the cluster heat map. *The American Statistician, 63*(2), 179–184.

Zeichner, K. M., Grant, C., Geneva, G., Gillette, M., Valli, L., & Villegas, A. M. (1998). A research informed vision of good practice in multicultural teacher education: Design principles. *Theory Into Practice, 37*(2), 163–171.

Stuart Henderson is the associate director for the Schools of Health Research Education Outcomes Evaluation Unit at the University of California, Davis. He has over 12 years of experience conducting qualitative research and is currently the Program Chair for the American Evaluation Association's Data Visualization and Reporting Topical Interest Group.

Eden H. Segal is a research analyst and project manager at Westat, a social science research and evaluation organization near Washington, DC. Her current work focuses on qualitative and mixed-method evaluations for foundations and federal, state, and local government organizations, primarily in education, health, and law.

Kistler, S. J., Evergreen, S., & Azzam, T. (2013). Toolography. In T. Azzam & S. Evergreen (Eds.), *Data visualization, part 1. New Directions for Evaluation, 139*, 73–84.

Toolography

Susan J. Kistler, Stephanie Evergreen, Tarek Azzam

Abstract

This chapter offers descriptions of a selection of the tools mentioned in this issue and the next, as well as others in use in the field, and provides readers with a general estimate of their ease of use, whether they are available for free, and their strengths and weaknesses, along with information on how to access further information and alternatives to the tool. The number of tools available for data visualization is both extensive and growing rapidly. We will look at example tools in several categories—data visualization suites, mapping tools, finishing tools, qualitative visualization tools, word cloud generators, and social network analysis tools—but want to reiterate that these are only a starting point. © Wiley Periodicals, Inc., and the American Evaluation Association.

Data Visualization Suites

Some products offer a suite of tools specifically designed for data visualization or data exploration. These are multifaceted programs with a host of tools integrated into a single package. Some, such as Tableau, are meant for use with any data set, whereas others, such as Google Public Data Explorer, were developed not with data visualization as the purpose, but to increase understanding of particular data sets.

Google Fusion Tables

Ease-of-use rating (1 = *very easy*, 5 = *very hard*): 1–3.

Free: Yes.

Strengths: Google Fusion Tables is a Web-based application used to graph public data found via Google. It excels at cross-referencing data from two or more data sets. Users who have Google Apps can also upload their own data sets. The resulting graphs and maps are interactive, in that the variables can be filtered and data points reveal details with a hover. Visualizations can be embedded in a website or distributed with a link. No programming expertise is needed to produce data displays at a simple level, but understanding basic programming significantly extends the capacity of Google Fusion Tables. Data are not made public.

Weaknesses: Graph layout types are very limited and pre-selected based on data, and colors are not customizable. Inappropriate pie charts with far too many slices are a default option. Fusion Tables is still a beta program with Google, meaning features and functions could change any time.

Help: Google Fusion Tables Help is a clear, easy-to-navigate help guide that also includes a forum for posting questions not already answered (http://support.google.com/fusiontables/?hl=en). Poynter features instructions on how to make a heat map in Fusion Tables (http://www.poynter.org/how-tos/digital-strategies/126628/how-to-make-a-heatmap-in-google-fusion-tables/).

Alternative Programs: Many Eyes, Tableau.

Google's Public Data Explorer

Ease-of-use rating (1 = *very easy*, 5 = *very hard*): 3.

Free: Yes.

Strengths: Google's Public Data Explorer is a Web-based application that lets users explore specific public data sets on world development indicators from such sources as the World Bank, U.S. Bureau of Labor Statistics, and the U.S. Census Bureau. Visualizations are available as line graphs, bar charts, maps, and scatterplots. Exploration of public data is point-and-click. Data filtering is clear and specific. No programming expertise is needed to produce data displays. Data displays can be embedded on websites or distributed via a link.

Weaknesses: Users can upload their own data set but specific metatags are required, which influence the ease-of-use rating for this tool. Some data filters are not defined well (e.g., less developed countries vs. more developed countries). Colors and fonts are not customizable. Built-in chart layouts can be insufficient. Producing graphs as picture files for slideshows or reports is not obvious and saving specific visualizations is not available.

Help: The Dataset Publishing Language (DSPL) will have to be used for users who upload their own data (https://developers.google.com/public-data/).

Alternative programs: Unknown.

Many Eyes

Ease-of-use rating (1 = *very easy*, 5 = *very hard*): 1.
Free: Yes.

Strengths: This suite of Web-based tools was created by IBM as a free test bed for using and sharing different visualizations. It is designed to be very user friendly and can create quantitative and qualitative visualizations including tree maps, phrase nets, basic GIS maps, bubble charts—over 15 different types of visualizations in all. The suite was built on the premise that if data are shared freely and multiple people can analyze it and visualize it in different ways, then this increases knowledge generation. Each visualization type includes specific information on when to use it and the data requirements.

Weaknesses: Data sets used on Many Eyes must be made public, preventing use for any data with identifying information for which privacy or confidentiality is a consideration. In addition, most of the tools, such as those for GIS and network analysis, offer few options with which to conduct a deeper level of analysis, having traded off ease of use for depth of features.

Help: The website is designed to be very user friendly, with step-by-step instructions on how to upload and create visualizations (http://www-958 .ibm.com/software/analytics/manyeyes/page/Tour.html).

Alternative programs: Because of the range of tools available, alternatives depend on which functionality is in use.

Microsoft Excel

Ease-of-use rating (1 = *very easy*, 5 = *very hard*): 2.
Free: No.

Strengths: Excel is a widely used quantitative analysis program, developed on a stable platform, with a long history and relatively easy integration with other Microsoft Office products. It both houses quantitative data and creates visualizations in multiple variations of column, line, pie, bar, area, scatter, and other types of graphs. Colors are infinitely customizable and a wide variety of fonts are available. Chart layouts are built into the software. No programming expertise is needed to produce data displays. Data displays can be exported or saved in a variety of formats, including as pictures, and can be easily transferred to other Microsoft Office software programs. Multiple add-ins available.

Weaknesses: Built-in chart layouts can be insufficient. Sometimes textboxes must be overlaid to place labels in appropriate positions. In some cases, data must be arranged in precise formats in order for the visualization to display properly, which can take some guesswork. Interactivity and drill-down ability with visualizations are limited. Ability to publish to the Web is not straightforward.

NEW DIRECTIONS FOR EVALUATION • DOI: 10.1002/ev

Further information: Microsoft Office Help has video tutorials available, with varying quality. For a good example, see the tutorial on making sparklines. For a bad example, see the video on Create a Chart (http://office.microsoft.com/en-us/excel/excel-skills-builderlearn-how-to-create-spreadsheets-and-workbooks-use-formulas-and-perform-data-analysis-FX102592909.aspx?WT.mc_id=eml_enus_RM-ExcelSkillsBuilder_GetFreeButton). Mr. Excel has comprehensive articles with step-by-step instructions online. Related e-book available for purchase. Consulting services available (http://www.mrexcel.com/).

Alternative programs: Google Spreadsheet, OpenOffice.

Tableau

Ease-of-use rating (1 = *very easy*, 5 = *very hard*): 3.

Free: Yes for data sets that may be made public, no for private data sets.

Strengths: Providing a host of tools for visualization of quantitative data, Tableau encourages data exploration and facilitates the creation of interactive data visualizations with the capacity to filter and drill down to explore questions of interest. Its friendly user interface makes it easy to get started, and intelligent data integration and identification limits selections to visualizations that are feasible for your data. The paid version integrates well and in real time with multiple data sources and data types.

Weaknesses: Although it is easy to get started, learning the full set of features takes time and effort. Like Many Eyes, the free version requires making your data public, and the relatively expensive standard desktop version does not allow for online sharing of interactive visualizations. The product's laser focus on data visualization means that even simple quantitative analyses such as to generate derived variables are easier for the beginner to do prior to importation of a data set.

Further information: Tableau has extensive manuals, an online knowledge base of searchable questions and answers, step-by-step video tutorials, and an active user community at http://www.tableausoftware.com/support

Alternative programs: Unknown.

Mapping Tools

A range of tools allow users to integrate geographic and nongeographic data. Mapping tools such as Bing Maps and Google Maps allow users to annotate a map with location information like details about program sites, facilitating visualization of site and location changes over time. With the addition of geographic information systems (GIS) functionality, we achieve integration of mapping and data sets as described in more detail in Part 2.

Bing Maps

Ease-of-use rating (1 = *very easy*, 5 = *very hard*): 2.

Free: Yes.

Strengths: Maps produced via Bing Maps can be shared with others and can be used to depict changes in program outcomes by modifying the color of the location icons. These maps can also be embedded into websites and used as part of a dashboard. As a Microsoft product, it is not surprising that Bing Maps integrates well with Microsoft Office, in particular with Excel through the Bing Maps app for Office that generates limited map-based data visualizations within Excel.

Weaknesses: Compared to Google Maps, Bing Maps is generally less comprehensive. For example, it does not allow for the importing of GIS data files (i.e., KML), its street view option is limited to specific geographic regions, and it is not as well designed for collaboration.

Help: Microsoft offers a good introduction to the use of Bing Maps (http://onlinehelp.microsoft.com/en-us/bing/ff808582.aspx).

Alternative programs: ArcGIS, Google Maps.

Google Maps

Ease-of-use rating (1 = *very easy*, 5 = *very hard*): 1.

Free: Yes.

Strengths: Google Maps offers a collaboration feature that allows collaborators to work on the creation of a map and allows users to upload GIS data files (i.e., KML) if needed. Another important feature is the ability to link to other websites and to embed the maps across different platforms (e.g., Microsoft and Apple). A very active user forum offers many suggestions and opportunities for creative solutions to issues and problems. The coverage of certain features, such as street view, is also more comprehensive than similar sites (i.e., Bing Maps).

Weaknesses: Compared to ArcGIS, Google Maps only allows users to conduct a descriptive level of analysis and does not allow for the easy layering of data on top of the map.

Further information: Google offers a help menu with many resources about getting started and access to an active user community (http://support.google.com/maps/?hl=en).

Alternative programs: ArcGIS, Bing Maps.

ArcGIS

Ease-of-use rating (1 = *very easy*, 5 = *very hard*): 4.

Free: No.

Strengths: ArcGIS from ESRI is the most widely adopted GIS analysis software in the world. ArcGIS is very comprehensive, allowing users to conduct geostatistical analysis to create complex maps and conduct inferential analysis on the geographic variables while sharing maps online. ArcGIS integrates well with geographic databases. This software is also moving towards a web-based interface similar to Google Maps that allows users to upload their own data to map it (this is in the early stages of development). ArcGIS also has an extensive support community to help with complex maps and analysis. Many GIS trainings tend to focus on ArcGIS, because it is so widely adopted.

Weaknesses: ArcGIS is expensive and typically requires an annual subscription to access the more advanced features. Its extensive and complex features set creates a steep learning curve for the user to master some of the fundamental concepts. Many of the features are also not useful for social scientists, because ArcGIS was originally designed for geographers.

Further information: ESRI provides a detailed help webpage with resource links and tutorials (http://webhelp.esri.com/arcgisdesktop/9.2/index.cfm?TopicName=welcome).

Alternative programs: CartoDB, Google Earth, GRASS GIS, Quantum GIS.

Finishing Tools

A whole host of tools allows the user to work with visualizations to perfect layout or appearance and/or add interactivity for online content. These tools do not generate data-based visualizations (or that is not their strength) so much as they refine visualizations generated elsewhere or create visualizations as an artist would, from scratch.

Adobe Illustrator

Ease-of-use rating (1 = *very easy*, 5 = *very hard*): 4.
Free: No.
Strengths: Adobe Illustrator is software commonly used by designers. Users can import data visualizations from Excel or other platforms for manipulation of font, color, and so on. Limited charting is available in the software by pasting a table of data. Sometimes designers will use the drawing tools to draw a graph, rather than use one based on actual data. Colors are infinitely customizable. A wide variety of fonts are available. No programming expertise is needed. Data displays can be saved in a variety of formats, including as pictures, and easily transferred to other programs.
Weaknesses: The learning curve to get proficient enough to work with graphs is fairly steep. The software is not free. To manipulate parts of a graph based on actual data, users must break the graph pieces apart, which cannot be undone; thus all other alterations to the graph must be completely considered and executed in advance.
Further information: Nathan Yau has a straightforward blog post on how to make graphs in Adobe Illustrator (http://flowingdata.com/2008/12/16/how-to-make-a-graph-in-adobe-illustrator/).
Alternative programs: GIMP, Inkscape.

Adobe Flash

Ease-of-use rating (1 = *very easy*, 5 = *very hard*): 4.
Free: No.

Strengths: Adobe Flash is often used to create interactive website content. The software allows users to create multiple layers of content that is linked to pictures, videos, or other websites. It can be used to create interactive program theories that allow for multiple layers of detail and complexity. The flash file that is produced at the end of this process can be embedded into websites and PowerPoint for sharing and communication purposes.

Weaknesses: The learning curve is steep and requires training and some knowledge of programming. There is also a growing trend away from Flash-based content (e.g., Flash is not supported on Apple products) to HTML5 language. The Flash objects can also be unstable in PowerPoint and the price of the software is high.

Further information: The Adobe Flash help website contains many resources, including a community blog and video tutorials (http://helpx. adobe.com/flash.html).

Alternative programs: Swishmax 4 (much cheaper).

Qualitative Visualization Tools

The tools available for qualitative visualization are dwarfed by their quantitative cousins, yet are expanding as new tools come on the market and older tools add visualization functionality.

MAXQDA

Ease-of-use rating (1 = *very easy*, 5 = *very hard*): 3.
Free: No.
Strengths: MAXQDA is a qualitative analysis software package with some visualization capacity. Qualitative data can be visualized as a network map, bar chart, simple matrix displays, concept maps, color-coded "text portraits," and tag clouds. Users have many color choices and can customize nodes on network with photos or other images. MAXQDA also used multiple visualizations internal to the program as part of data exploration and analysis, including code matrices, and thematic and relationship visualizations that may be drilled into interactively to explore the underlying data.

Weaknesses: MAXQDA is not yet available for Mac computers. Many of the visualizations used for data exploration are not easily interpretable by those unfamiliar with MAXQDA. As with most qualitative visualization tools, the functionality is relatively new and being refined.

Further information: In-program help is supplemented by an extensive and searchable frequently asked questions (FAQ) website and active user discussion forum (http://www.maxqda.com/support/need-help-look-here-for-a-quick-solution).

Alternative programs: Atlast.ti, NVivo.

NVivo

Ease-of-use rating (1 = *very easy*, 5 = *very hard*): 3.

Free: No.

Strengths: QSR's NVivo is a long-standing qualitative analysis software package with expanded visualization capacity added in recent upgrades. Qualitative data can be visualized with the use of tag clouds, tree maps, word trees, and connection maps; as well as quantitative column, pie, and bar charts based on frequency data. Visualizations can be customized, albeit limited, and are exportable in multiple formats. NVivo is available for both Mac and PC platforms.

Weaknesses: Many of the visualizations used for data exploration are not easily interpretable by those unfamiliar with NVivo. As with most qualitative visualization tools, the functionality is relatively new and being refined.

Further information: In-program help is supplemented by an extensive and searchable FAQ website and active user discussion forum (http://www.qsrinternational.com/support.aspx).

Alternative programs: Atlast.ti, MAXQDA.

Word Cloud Generators

Word clouds take a body of text and generate a cloud of words, with each word sized based on frequency. The word cloud in Figure 4.1 shows the text from the *Guiding Principles for Evaluators* wrapped around the American Evaluation Association logo with the use of Tagxedo.com. The most ubiquitous word cloud generator is Wordle, which is also used as the basis for the cloud generator in Many Eyes. Although not a data analysis tool per se, word clouds are useful in evaluation reporting and as prompts during interviews or group discussions.

Wordle

Ease-of-use rating (1 = *very easy*, 5 = *very hard*): 1.

Free: Yes.

Strengths: Wordle generates a word cloud based on either text or a URL, pasted into the Wordle webpage. Words that shouldn't be visualized (e.g., *the, a, and*) can be excluded. Limited fonts, colors, and layouts are available. Visualizations can be translated into many other languages and can be used commercially without credit to Wordle.

Weaknesses: Visualizations can be printed (tricky on a Mac), embedded on a website, or saved to a public gallery with a link for distribution, but other export formats are not available. The formula for linking word size to frequency is mysterious and doesn't always appear to work properly. The largest size is governed such that size can be misleading.

New Directions for Evaluation • DOI: 10.1002/ev

Figure 4.1. Example Word Cloud Based on Text From the
Guiding Principles for Evaluators **Prepared by Susan Kistler**
With the Use of Tagxedo

Further information: Wordle's FAQ has answers to everything from linking words into phrases to changing the size of the image (http://www .wordle.net/faq). Other information can be found in McNaught and Lam (2010).

Alternative programs: TagCrowd, Tagxedo.

Tagxedo

Ease-of-use rating (1 = *very easy*, 5 = *very hard*): 2.

Free: Yes.

Strengths: Tagxedo generates word clouds, based on text, a URL, a Twitter or Del.icio.us ID, keywords (which are then searched via a common search engine), or an RSS feed, that the user pastes into the Tagxedo webpage. Alternatively, the user may upload a text file. Excluded words, fonts, color schemes, and the sizing algorithm are all highly customizable and users can upload a custom shape for word wrapping. Word clouds generated in Tagxedo may be saved in multiple formats and resolutions. Visualizations are licensed under a Creative Commons Attribution-Noncommercial-ShareAlike license and must reference tagxedo.com as the origin.

Weaknesses: Tagxedo is built on the free Silverlight platform; some users may need to install Silverlight prior to use. Using the wide range of customization options takes some experimentation, in particular when customizing the sizing algorithm.

Further information: Tagxedo's FAQ has explanations of everything, from the many customizing options to why Tagxedo was built on the Silverlight platform (http://www.tagxedo.com/faq.html).

Alternative programs: TagCrowd, Wordle.

Social Network Analysis Tools

These tools create a visual representation of the connections between and among units such as people or organizations. The unit becomes a node and connections, such as reciprocal agreements or stakeholder relationships, are represented by lines or "edges" connecting the nodes (see Figure 4.2).

Netdraw

Ease-of-use rating (1 = *very easy*, 5 = *very hard*): 4.
Free: Yes.
Strengths: Netdraw from UCINET is one of the most popular tools for visualizing social network data. Size of nodes, color, and shape can be adjusted, though there are a limited range of options. No programming skills are required. The diagram can be saved as a picture file for distribution. Spanish language resources are available.

Weaknesses: Netdraw runs on a Windows platform, limiting usability for those using other operating systems. The learning curve can be quite steep and documentation is limited. Users must have a clear understanding of the necessary structure of the underlying spreadsheet as well as the various operations within the program to produce a visualization.

Further information: UCINET has an active users' group, which is the best place to post messages and help others (http://tech.groups.yahoo.com/group/ucinet/).

Alternative programs: Commetrix, Gephi, Node XL.

NodeXL

Ease-of-use rating (1 = *very easy*, 5 = *very hard*): 3.
Free: Yes (but there is a cost for Microsoft Excel).

Figure 4.2. Example Network Visualization Based on Those Using the Hashtag #eval on Twitter, Prepared by Susan Kistler With the Use of NodeXL

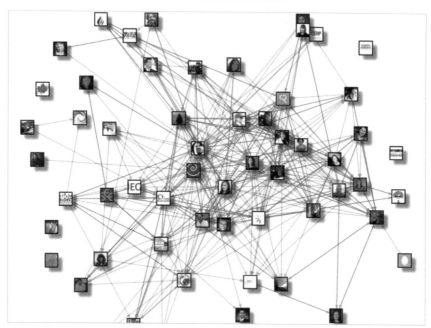

Strengths: NodeXL is an open-source template for Microsoft Excel. Built to extend the functionality of the Excel platform, its underlying user interface will be commonplace for many users. NodeXL features automatic integration with social media platforms such as Twitter and Facebook, and is a strong choice for visualizing connections within social media accounts, although it may be used for analyses of any networks. The forms of nodes and edges are highly customizable.

Weaknesses: Although extensive documentation is available, the learning curve is steep and users need to be familiar with the language and concepts of social network analysis to use the tool. Export of final graphs is limited.

Further information: NodeXL has extensive built-in documentation and an active discussion group at http://nodexl.codeplex.com/discussions. Also see Hansen, Shneiderman, and Smith (2010).

Alternative programs: Commetrix, Gephi, Netdraw.

References

Hansen, D., Shneiderman, B., & Smith, M. (2010). *Analyzing social media networks with NodeXL: Insights from a connected world*. Burlington, MA: Morgan Kaufmann.

McNaught, C., & Lam, P. (2010). *Using Wordle as a supplementary research tool*. Retrieved from http://www.nova.edu/ssss/QR/QR15–3/mcnaught.pdf

SUSAN J. KISTLER is the executive director of the American Evaluation Association and the owner of iMeasureMedia. She has shepherded AEA's evolution over the past 10 years through an era of technological evolution to where it is at the forefront of associations its size in terms of adoption and leveraging technology and social media in pursuit of its mission and goals.

STEPHANIE EVERGREEN is an evaluator who runs Evergreen Data, a data presentation consulting firm.

TAREK AZZAM is an assistant professor at Claremont Graduate University, and associate director of the Claremont Evaluation Center.

NEW DIRECTIONS FOR EVALUATION • DOI: 10.1002/ev

INDEX